EMPLOYMENT LAW
for the
SMALL BUSINESS

EMPLOYMENT LAW for the SMALL BUSINESS

Anne Knell

Published in association with
The Institute of Chartered Accountants
In England and Wales

KOGAN
PAGE

Copyright © Anne Knell 1989

All rights reserved. No reproduction, copy or transmission of this publication may be made without written permission.

No paragraph of this publication may be reproduced, copied or transmitted save with written permission or in accordance with the provisions of the Copyright Act 1956 (as amended), or under the terms of any licence permitting limited copying issued by the Copyright Licensing Agency, 7 Ridgmount Street, London WC1E 7AE.

Any person who does any unauthorised act in relation to this publication may be liable to criminal prosecution and civil claims for damages.

First published in Great Britain in 1989 by Kogan Page Limited, 120 Pentonville Road, London N1 9JN.

British Library Cataloguing in Publication Data

Knell, Anne
   Employment law for the small business.
   1. Great Britain. Employment law. For small
   firms
   I. Title
   344.104'1125

   ISBN 1-85091-713-2
   ISBN 1-85091-714-0 pbk

Printed and bound in Great Britain by
Biddles Limited, Guildford

Contents

1 Recruiting Staff   9

Becoming an employer 9; Planning for recruitment 9; Employees or self-employed? 10; The selection process 11; Discrimination in recruitment 19; Other aspects of the law in recruitment 25; Making a job offer 31; The induction process 33; Record keeping 34; Summary 35

2 Contract of Employment   36

Entitlement 36; Exclusions 36; Putting terms in writing 36; Definitions 37; What must be included in a written statement 41; Other provisions in the written terms and conditions 45; Implied terms and conditions 48; Custom and practice 49; Varying the terms of employment 49; Summary 50; Specimen contract for clerical and administrative staff 50; The firm's disciplinary procedure 55; Health and safety at work policy 57

3 Statutory Rights in Employment   58

Eligibility 58; Main entitlements 58; Guarantee payments 58; Medical suspension pay 59; Maternity rights 60; Public duties 63; Rights in insolvency 64; Transfer of undertakings regulations 65; Equal pay 66; Statutory sick pay 68

4   Paying People 76

Deciding how much to pay 76; Deciding the basis on which payment will be made 79; How and how often to pay 81; Summary 82; Checklist of PAYE forms 83

5   Employee Relations 91

The role of trade unions 91; Certificate of independence 91; Trade union recognition 92; What to include in a recognition agreement 93; Single union agreements 94; Rights of an independent trade union 97; Rights of individual employees and trade union membership 98; Possible stages of trade union recognition 98; Employee involvement initiatives 99; Trade disputes 102; Picketing 103; Strikes and the contract of employment 103; Resolution of industrial disputes 104; Payment during a strike 105; Continuous employment 105

6   Health and Safety at Work 106

The Health and Safety at Work Act *1974* 106; Employment Medical Advisory Service 113; Safety representatives 113; Safety policies 114; First-aid 114; Notices which must be displayed by the employer 120; Notification of injuries, diseases and dangerous occurrences 121; Health and safety legislation 127

7   Terminating Employment 129

The employee gives notice 129; Exit interviews 131; When the employer wishes to terminate employment 131; Giving notice 132; The right to go to an industrial tribunal 133; Dismissal for lack of capability or lack of qualifications 133; Dismissal for misconduct 135; Dismissal for redundancy 137; Dismissal for some other statutory reason 141; Dismissal for some other substantial reason 141; Automatically unfair dismissal 141; Contract frustration 142; Other reasons for termination of employment 143; Written reason for dismissal 145; Remedies for unfair dismissal 145; Summary 148; Industrial tribunals 148

8 *Government Bodies and Employment* **154**

The Department of Employment 154; Advisory, Conciliation and Arbitration Service 155; Industrial tribunals 156; Employment Appeal Tribunal 157; The Central Arbitration Committee 157; The Health and Safety Commission and the Health and Safety Executive 158; The Training Agency 158; Industrial Training Boards 159; The Equal Opportunities Commission and the Commission for Racial Equality 160; The Data Protection Registrar 162; Certification Officer 163; Wages Councils 164; Initiatives for dealing with unemployment 164

Appendices

1 Forms Required by Law *169*
2 Recommended Reading *174*
3 Useful Addresses *176*

Index 179

1
Recruiting Staff

Becoming an employer

Once your business begins to grow you will no longer be able to carry out on your own all the tasks which have to be done, and you will need to recruit others to help. It can often be tempting to invite people you know who are seeking employment to come and join, often in an undefined and unstructured role. The reasoning is that another pair of hands can always be given something useful to do; Jill, who was made redundant by a local company, or Bill, who is semi-retired but wants something to occupy his time, must surely have skills which will be of value to a growing business. And so they may have. Sometimes those arrangements work well for a period and then become a more formal employer/employee relationship. Very often, however, they end in dissatisfaction all round because both parties look for something in the relationship which was never intended to be there.

As the business grows, the owner (by now an employer) looks for more conformity, more systems, introduces more rules. Bill is happy to do 20 or so hours a week, but when *he* wants to do it. Suddenly the needs of each party cannot be satisfied by what the other has to offer, so there is a parting of the ways, often acrimonious and accusatory. (It is even worse to let the situation fester, with the employer becoming more and more frustrated at what is not being done but not liking to say anything because he or she doesn't want to upset Bill who was so useful in the early days.) Managing other people is never easy, which makes it all the more important to start out with well defined tasks for employees to do and, where possible, a clear idea of the level of performance which you consider to be satisfactory.

Planning for recruitment

To avoid such problems, as far as possible, it is essential that planning for recruitment is carried out as meticulously as any other aspect of business planning. The process starts in fact with the business plan. You have identified what you can realistically hope to achieve in one, three or five years. You have defined what you will be doing (eg producing table mats) or the services you will be offering (eg executive lunches). You now have to translate these plans into the skills you will need to make them happen. Group the skills together in logical clusters, and you begin to define discrete jobs. You have to decide where your own skills lie and in which aspects of the business you want to be actively involved. If you are an inventive genius, you may need help in administration and marketing. If you are good at production and engineering, you may need assistance in identifying sales opportunities. Some skills you will need because all businesses require them (basic accounting for instance); some will be necessary because of the business you have chosen (you cannot manufacture without production skills); other skills will be needed because they supplement your own.

Employees or self-employed?

Once you have defined what needs to be done, it is worth considering whether you actually need to hire people or whether you could do better by buying in the skills as and when you need them. Accounting services can be purchased, sales agents will act on your behalf without becoming employees, bureaux will process data, cleaning contractors will look after your premises. There is an army of firms or self-employed people who between them offer most of the services you are likely to need.

The decision ultimately has to balance cost and convenience. If you are employing two people, you do not need a personnel manager. Some advice on contracts of employment or statutory sick pay regulations might, however, be very useful. So you hire in the advice when you need it. Although it may sometimes appear expensive it is a one-off, manageable cost which remains firmly within your control. You are not paying an annual salary to someone for their professional expertise which is hardly ever needed. Once you are employing 200 people, however, it will probably be more cost-effective to bring the function in-house and recruit someone to do what your consultants have been doing previously.

The disadvantages of not recruiting your own staff are mainly to do with flexibility and convenience. Consultants, auditors, advisers, even cleaners, are not on call all the time (or if they are there is a large premium to pay for such a facility). Nor can you easily ask the accountant who is doing your monthly management accounts if he minds emptying the waste bins and running a duster round the office before he goes! However, your own employees, particularly where they feel involved in the business, will often help out in a variety of tasks when the need for their own particular skills is slack. If you do decide to hire in skills as and when you need them, make sure that there is a proper contract which specifies what will be done for you, how, when and how much it will cost, and make sure that you have the right to terminate that contract with reasonable notice. This is a contract for services, not a contract of employment.

The selection process

A person specification

Once you have made the decision to recruit, it is important to set about it in a logical way. You have already defined what you want to be done. Formalise this by writing up a job specification which lists the purpose of the job and its main tasks. Then translate this into the kind of person you feel will be most successful in the post. A good framework for defining the person you are looking for is the Seven Point Plan. Under each of the headings listed below, decide what attributes your employee *must* have, and which are merely desirable. If you say something is essential, this implies that candidates who lack it will not even get as far as the interview. The seven points are:

Physical characteristics
Dress, appearance, health and age are all considerations here. Important factors may be physical strength or ability to manage heights or withstand heat, or freedom from allergies etc if the job holder will be working with detergents or chemicals. A non-smoker may be preferred for safety reasons.

Attainments
Are any educational or professional qualifications needed? What kind of experience should the successful candidate bring to the business?

General intelligence
Are you looking for someone capable of conceptual thought, or simply someone who will bring common sense to bear on everyday problems?

Special aptitudes
Should candidates be good at arithmetic, able to write elegant letters, skilled in persuading people to buy, or able to write computer programs? Should they be good with their hands and at understanding how things work?

Interests
Are there essential elements of the work in which candidates must be interested if they are to find real job satisfaction? Are there activities outside work which might be useful indicators of the sort of skills the candidate might have?

Disposition
What kind of interpersonal skills are you looking for? Must the candidate be able to persuade others, be a decision-maker or a follower, play a leading role in a team or be content to be told what to do? Will he or she work with a lot of other people, and if so how important is it to get on with them? Will he or she have to sell to particularly difficult customers and, if so, what attributes will be needed to be acceptable?

Circumstances
Must people be available to work shifts, unsocial hours, travel away from home a lot etc?

Once you have defined all these factors, you are ready to look for your candidates.

Advertising
The most important consideration of any method of looking for staff is that it is cost-effective. A large display advertisement in the *Daily Telegraph* may bring many replies, but if the candidate you are looking for probably lives within five miles of your business, and you are unwilling to pay relocation costs, then a smaller advertisement in the local paper (which will be a fraction of the cost) will meet your needs better. The good advertisement is not the one which brings in 200 replies; it is the one which finds the

right candidate, even if only one person responds.

A good advertisement follows a number of simple rules:

- it is clearly and cleanly laid out with well defined borders;
- the job title is unambiguous and large enough to attract attention;
- the company is mentioned by name – if this is impossible it may be better to use an agency or consultant to carry out the preliminary search for you; box numbers cut the potential response considerably;
- brief details of the job are given, clarifying the duties of the job holder;
- a précis of the employee specification is included, so that potential candidates can measure themselves against your requirements and not waste their time or yours in applying if they do not meet your minimum needs;
- the rewards of the post are stated. This means that you do not attract replies from those who are looking for twice as much as you want to pay or are only earning half of the salary you feel is right for the job. Neither group of people is likely to be right for the position you are offering;
- the way you would prefer people to apply is clearly given. If you invite candidates to telephone for a preliminary talk you must clear your diary of other matters for the two or so days following the advertisement; candidates will tend to drop out if they can never get to talk to you because you are out or in a meeting. The best form of response is usually to ask for details of previous employment etc to be sent in writing so that you can assess the response at your leisure. This allows you to control the time, not the candidates.

Your company is being judged by every step you take once an advertisement has appeared. This makes it very important to treat all candidates with courtesy, responding to applications as quickly as possible, even if sending only a 'holding' letter.

Other ways of attracting candidates

Advertising is not the only means of attracting candidates, however. You might consider the use of

- Employment agencies. These are especially useful for secretarial and clerical staff in cities and large towns where

potential candidates find it convenient to go into an agency which will seek a job for them rather than respond to newspaper advertisements. Fees are normally payable only when a candidate is successfully placed with you.
- Recruitment consultants, particularly for management level posts. These consultants will normally spend time with you finding out exactly what you are looking for, will advise on salary and benefits, advertise on your behalf and interview an initial shortlist, and present you with a final shortlist of three or so candidates. Many of them can offer a range of psychometric tests to supplement the interview information. Fees are normally payable whether or not the process is successful, but you should always ensure before you engage consultants that you have a copy of their terms and conditions and that you understand what you are committing yourself to. The advantage from your point of view is that you are paying for a highly professional service carried out by those whose job it is to interview and assess people. It is only a small part of *your* normal daily activities, and the more successful you are at choosing the right people the less often you should need to do it. It is easy to get out of the habit of good, structured interviews and begin to rely on impressions instead. A professional look at a candidate can save your time and money in the longer run.
- Executive search or head-hunters. This method is most useful if the post really is a 'top' one paying a salary in excess of £50,000, or if the kind of person you seek is so rare that he or she needs to be prised away from an existing employer by careful persuasion. The cost is high – usually not less than 33 per cent of starting salary – and some firms of executive search will not accept assignments without specifying a minimum fee level. Again, it is important to ensure that you have a copy of the terms of business and understand exactly what you will get for your money.

Methods of finding staff do not have to be expensive. For unskilled, semi-skilled and skilled employees in offices or factories a 'Vacancies Board' outside the place of work can often attract local people. The Jobcentre and local disablement officer will provide help and candidates free of charge, although the Professional and Executive Register (PER), which was the managerial arm of the Department of Employment's jobs service, charge a fee like any other agency and has just been bought by Pergamon

Press. Word of mouth can also be effective in a small community, but if you rely on this to provide a steady stream of applicants it is important to ensure that you are not unwittingly offending the discrimination laws. These are discussed later in this chapter.

Using the right selection method

Whatever method of looking for candidates you have used, once you have attracted responses you should first compare the candidates with your employee specification and reject those who do not meet your essential criteria. The others should then be assessed against the desirable criteria, and those who clearly conform to your requirements invited along for assessment.

The interview

The main method of selection used is the interview. This is because it has most face validity – it is what people expect and they are happy to be judged by their interview performance. It also offers a good means for exchanging information – the candidates about themselves and you about the company and the job on offer. However, as a means of arriving at an accurate assessment of a person it has many defects, including our in-built prejudices (of all kinds, not only confined to race and sex) and the lack of experience and competence of many interviewers.

The good interview is the one where the candidate does most of the talking in response to your skilful questions, not the one where you spend two hours expanding on how you started out with nothing and built up an empire. That can wait until you are sure the applicant is the right person to come and help you run that empire.

Imperfect as it is, the interview is nevertheless likely to remain the central point of any selection process. It is important therefore to use it as effectively as possible. If you foresee that you will spend a considerable time interviewing potential staff, it would be a worthwhile investment to get some professional training in interviewing skills. There are many courses available which will reinforce the theory of interviewing with practical skills. Most managers can be taught to be competent interviewers and avoid the obvious pitfalls of this method of assessing candidates.

The ground-rules of successful interviewing are simple, though not so easy to apply without guidance and experience. The most important are:

- *Be prepared.* The candidate has spent time and effort in

putting together a CV for you to read. Use it before the interview in planning the shape of your meeting with him or her. Ask yourself:
- where should I begin the interview – with the present job, education, interests etc? As a general rule, the most relevant aspect of a candidate's background will be the job he or she is proposing to leave in order to join you. The candidate will therefore expect to be asked about it and will feel relaxed once he or she is able to start talking about something familiar. There are no hard and fast rules – you must use your judgement. It is hardly appropriate to begin an interview with a 50-year-old man by asking him what his favourite subjects at school were, but this may be the best place to start with a 17-year-old.
- from the written application, where is the evidence which suggests that the candidate has the skills I need and how can I best explore that evidence to ensure that it really is relevant to this job?
- are there any areas where I feel relevant experience may be lacking, and how can I ask about this without provoking the wrong response from the candidate?
- what has the candidate omitted from the application which I need to know – health record or referees perhaps?
- is the information consistent and can I check any of it (eg a relevant professional qualification) before the interview, or should I ask for proof of qualifications etc to be brought to the interview?
- what information must I be sure to establish in the interview which may not appear in an application, eg possession of a valid driving licence if this is needed for the post, or whether or not the candidate is a smoker where this is not permitted at work?

- *Establish good rapport*. This begins before you even see the candidate. It can be fostered by ensuring that your receptionist or security person is given a note of the people who are expected so that they can be directed to the right place without delay, and that the waiting area is reasonably quiet so that the candidates are not the focus of all eyes as they wait for you. Something for them to read if they are early should be available (this can be a useful way of getting across information about the company through product brochures etc), and they should be given an opportunity to visit the washroom if they have travelled some way to see you. Most important of all, the interview should start on time. Where interview expenses are being paid, delegating the responsibility to the receptionist or your secretary can save you valuable time and put the candidate's mind at rest particularly if the fare has been an expensive one. Meeting the candidate in the reception area yourself is also useful and enables you to get through the preliminary chat as you walk back to your office or the interview room. If you normally run up three flights of stairs to prove how fit you are, do not expect or require candidates to do the same. Ensure that the room you are using for the interview is quiet, tidy and free from all interruptions, both by people and telephones. Candidates will not relax and tell you all about themselves if the door bursts open every two minutes with yet another person demanding your time or decision. Apart from the impossibility of getting enough information about the candidates in these circumstances, it also reflects badly on you if they feel that your style of management means that you have to make all the decisions. Rapport does not mean slapping candidates on the back and calling them by their first name within the first five minutes – some will be put off by this approach, preferring to advance to the use of first names more gradually.

- *Ask the right kind of questions.* The right questions are those which do not allow candidates to confine responses to 'yes' and 'no' but which require them to explain, describe, elaborate or justify. They are the questions which begin with 'What did you do next?', 'Why did you do that?', How did you accomplish this?', 'Which would you say . . . ?' If particular information you are looking for is not provided through these open questions, you may need to narrow them down a bit, eg 'Describe your supervisory experience.' If you are still not sure about specific points, ask a specific question: 'How many people were you actually responsible for?' Remember to start with the open questions, though, or you will find the interview turning into an inquisition as you ask more and more specific questions which need one-word answers, and where you have to work particularly hard to keep up the flow of questions. A good interview should be like a conversation with an interesting stranger, where you prompt the narrative with questions which direct the conversation and ensure that you get the information you need but which do not become intrusive and impede the flow of the conversation. You should avoid questions which imply the right answer, eg 'I think these new computer systems are a waste of time, don't you?' or which offer so many options to the candidate that he or she becomes confused.

- *Listen*. The greatest weakness of many interviewers is that they do not listen. They are so busy thinking of the next question or allowing their mind to drift while the candidates talk, worrying about what is happening on the shop floor, that they do not hear what is being said. In this way they could miss vital information which would allow them to make a proper assessment and at worst they could sometimes ask the same question several times.

- *Allow time for candidates to ask questions*. This is an essential part of the interview process; it can be quite revealing about the candidates' attitudes, what they feel strongly enough to ask questions about (How much holiday is there?) and may highlight doubts or worries about the job which had not previously been identified. It may also provide an opportunity for the candidate to reinforce aspects of experience which are relevant.

- *Check that you have all the information you need before you close the interview*. Once candidates have gone, it will be too late, without asking them back or telephoning them, to clarify any information which you did not understand at the time or probe an area where you were not satisfied that you had all the information you needed. The danger of not checking at the time is that you make a decision about candidates on incomplete information and may either assume wrongly or otherwise in their favour. In neither case is it fair to the candidates, who could have provided the correct information if asked.

- *Ask if there is anything the candidates wish to add*. This ensures that they have every chance to emphasise those parts of their experience which they feel are relevant, and reinforces their feeling that they have had a fair interview.

- *Ask if the candidates are still interested in the post.* While most candidates will probably say 'yes', this does provide another opportunity to check any doubts they may have and may give you some feedback on the way on which you have put your job across to them through the advertisement, job specification and interview. If candidates are no longer interested because the job is not what they thought it was, you may need to revise your description to bring it closer to reality.

- *Tell the candidates when they can expect to hear from you* – and make sure you stick to your timetable.

Other selection methods
There are other ways of assessing the suitability of candidates, the usefulness of which will depend on the nature of the job and how much additional information they will in fact contribute. First, any methods you use must provide relevant insights into the candidates or they are a waste of time and money. It is helpful if candidates can see the relevance as well as yourself. Second, you should believe that the methods you are using will predict success in the job. Third, you should ensure that the methods are valid in themselves – that is, they really do measure what they purport to measure. Finally, as with interviews, you should be trained in their use and interpretation before you begin to use them.

The most commonly used techniques fall into two categories:

- group selection procedures, where candidates meet each other and are assessed for their ability to get on with a group of their peers;
- tests and questionnaires which may measure a whole range of attributes and abilities from intelligence to interests.

Both can be of considerable benefit but both need to be used carefully.

Discrimination in recruitment
The procedures outlined above should be straightforward and, if properly monitored, should enable a company to check that it is

being effective in the way it sets about recruiting staff. It is, however, important that in applying these procedures and techniques you do not directly or indirectly discriminate against applicants on grounds of race, sex or marital status. The requirements are set out in the Sex Discrimination Acts 1975 and 1986 and the Race Relations Act 1976.

Direct discrimination
This is the name given to the exclusion of a category of candidates by simple reference to sex, race or marital status, eg 'No women need apply', 'Single men only'. Most discrimination is not so obvious but it is important to keep an open mind in drawing up an employee specification, wording an advertisement and choosing a shortlist, and not to imply by numerous references to 'him' and 'he' that the candidates will be men. It is also important not to fall into the trap of stereotyping jobs – 'bricklayers are men, secretaries are women' – but to take each application on its merit. All those in your company who come into contact with candidates should be aware of this – the first sex discrimination case was won by a man who was told by a telephonist that the job he was enquiring about was for women only.

Indirect discrimination
This occurs when you include in your employee specification a requirement for some attribute which all candidates must possess, which cannot be justified and which is to the detriment of one sex or the other, married persons, or those from ethnic minorities. If for example you had a vacancy for a cleaner, and specified that all candidates to be considered should be 6ft tall, this is a requirement which discriminates against women because the proportion of women who could comply with such a requirement, in the population as a whole, is smaller than the proportion of men. You are therefore indirectly discriminating against women; this is unlawful unless you can prove that being 6ft tall is absolutely essential for the proper execution of the job.

From this you can see that drawing up an employee specification has to be done with great care. All attributes have to be thought through and reliance on past practice should be minimised. There have been cases brought successfully to industrial tribunals where rejected candidates have been able to claim discrimination because the company has demanded good standards of spoken and written English. The tribunal argument was that this was irrelevant in a job consisting of sweeping the floor, ie the requirement was not justifiable and excluded from consideration many recent immigrants for whom English was not a first language. In another case, however, an applicant of Chinese origin, who was unable to pass a selection test requiring him to write a report on a piece of research, was found not to have been discriminated against because the test mirrored the job itself and the requirement was justifiable.

Non-discriminatory practices must therefore be extended through the whole of the selection process, from drawing up the employee specification to the type of selection techniques used. These must not exclude categories of applicants. If the ability to read and write English really is essential, then all candidates should be given the same test irrespective of race, colour, ethnic background or educational attainments. If certain levels of physical strength are needed to do a job, then both male and female applicants should be tested and not just the women.

The way in which you set about finding candidates should also be non-discriminatory. Using an agency or consultancy, to which all potential candidates have equal access, or advertising in the local or national press, will normally be non-discriminatory. Relying on word of mouth from the existing workforce may, however, lay you open to charges of discrimination unless your present workforce reflects the ethnic composition of the area from which you draw your employees. Equally, making apprenticeships available to sons of the existing workforce could be discriminatory in terms of race and sex.

The questions you ask in the interview should not be prejudiced. You should not assume that a woman with two children will be a less reliable employee than a single man and base your selection decision upon that unproven assumption. You should not assume that because a candidate's postal address is in an area where many people from ethnic minorities live that he or she will be a weak candidate and therefore decide, on that alone, that the candidate is not suitable for interview.

In effect, what the law requires you to do is to approach the selection process with criteria for choice of candidate which are justifiable in terms of the job and those who apply, based on the needs of the job and not predetermined assumptions and prejudice based on discrimination.

Genuine occupational qualifications

Both the Race Relations and Sex Discrimination Acts recognise that there are some jobs where being of a particular sex or race may be a justifiable requirement in itself. These genuine occupational qualifications (or GOQs) are very restrictive, however, and will be relevant to few commercial, professional or industrial companies.

GOQs – sex discrimination

The law permits you to require specifically a man or woman to do a particular job if it is for the following reasons:

- physiology, a modelling or acting job where the role requires a man or woman for reasons of authenticity;
- where the job involves physical contact with the opposite sex or working in a place where members of the opposite sex are likely to be in a state of undress;
- when the nature or location of the establishment makes it impractical for the employee to live other than on the premises provided by the employer *and* these do not provide separate accommodation and sanitary facilities for both sexes *and* it is not reasonable to expect the employer to so provide.
- if the work is in a single-sex prison, hospital or other special establishment;
- when the holder of the job provides individuals with personal services promoting their welfare or education and those services can most effectively be provided by a man or woman, eg social workers;
- where the law requires the employee to be of a particular sex;
- where the job involves working outside the UK in a country whose laws or customs are such that the duties could not, or could not effectively, be performed by a person of a specific sex;
- the job is one of those to be held by a married couple.

However, where there are already enough persons of the right sex in your employment to carry out all the jobs alleged to be GOQs, selection thereafter must be on a non-discriminatory basis. For example, if you own a men's outfitters and already employ two or three men who can carry out such tasks as measuring inside legs, it would be discriminatory to refuse to consider a woman for any additional posts as there would be other staff who could carry out the potentially sensitive tasks.

GOQs – race discrimination
These restrictions are even fewer and apply only where the job requires a person of a particular race or ethnic background for reasons of:

- authenticity in participation in a dramatic performance;
- authenticity in modelling;
- authenticity in places with a 'special ambience' where food or drink is served;
- providing persons of that racial group with personal services promoting their welfare, and where those services can best be provided by someone from the same racial group.

Again, where there are already sufficient persons of the particular racial group employed to carry out specific tasks, further recruitment should be on a non-discriminatory basis.

Neither in sex nor race discrimination is there any provision for an employer to choose specifically a man or woman, or a person from a particular ethnic group, in order to maintain a 'balanced' team.

The role of the industrial tribunal
If candidates feel that you have discriminated against them on the basis of sex, marital status or race, they can take a case to an industrial tribunal. In recruitment, the person concerned will have to put forward evidence that his or her non-selection was because of your discrimination but in doing so is allowed to ask for certain information to be revealed about the competition. In particular it may be asked, through the tribunal, that you disclose:

- the number of candidates;
- the age, education, qualifications and experience of those selected for interview;
- the criteria on which you based your selection decisions;
- the age, education, qualifications and experience of the selected candidate.

(The requirement not to discriminate applies to internal promotions and transfers as well. Your history of promoting women or people from ethnic minorities may then become admissable evidence before a tribunal.)

The tribunal will also consider how many women or people from ethnic minorities you already employ in similar posts and, with ethnic minorities, will also look at the proportions of people you employ in relation to the composition of the local area from which you draw your employees.

If the tribunal believes that you have discriminated against the candidate, either directly or indirectly, it will make an order for compensation and require you to amend your selection procedures so that future discrimination is avoided.

Codes of practice

Equal opportunities in employment are monitored by two statutory bodies: the Equal Opportunities Commission (EOC), which deals with sex discrimination and discrimination on grounds of marital status, and the Commission for Racial Equality (CRE), which deals with matters of race.

The composition and powers of both of these bodies is set out in Chapter 8. Where recruitment is concerned, however, both Commissions have produced codes of practice which should be followed by all employers. Failure to do so is not an offence in itself, but can be produced by a rejected candidate as strong evidence of an intention to discriminate.

In summary, the codes of practice recommend that you:

- decide the qualifications and experience needed (employee specification);
- consider internal transfer or promotion;
- obtain as much information about candidates as is relevant for selection and avoid asking for unnecessary information;
- make suitability for the job the selection criteria;
- check recruitment and selection methods from time to time to ensure that they are effective and not discriminatory;
- carry out occasional audits on the composition of applicants and successful candidates to ensure that discrimination is not taking place.

Equal opportunities and lack of discrimination are not just matters for consideration in recruitment, of course; other aspects are considered in Chapter 3.

Other aspects of the law in recruitment

There are some other laws which have to be taken into account when you decide to become an employer. The most important are listed below.

Employing children

A 'child' is someone who is under the age at which he or she is free in law to leave compulsory schooling. That age at present is 16. If you are thinking of taking on school-aged children for part-time work, there are a number of restrictions:

- the minimum age for employment is 13 years;
- you may not offer work during normal school hours on days when the child is expected to be at school;
- the children may not work before 7am or after 7pm;
- on days when they are required to attend school, or on Sundays, children may not work for more than two hours;
- they may not be required to move or lift anything which is so heavy that is is likely to cause them injury.

If you wish to employ a child you should obtain a permit from the local education authority, which has the right to ask you for further information about the employment you propose to offer.

Under the Education (Work Experience) Act 1973, children in their final year of compulsory education are allowed to undertake work experience as part of their education in line with arrangements either made or approved by the local education authority.

Employing 'young persons'

A 'young person' is less than 18 years old but has ceased to be a child, ie he or she is 16 or over. There are some general rules which must be observed at the present time. However, the 1988 Employment Bill aims to remove many of the following rules:

- hours of work in a week must not exceed 48, excluding meal breaks and rest periods;
- there are tighter restrictions on hours if the employment (whether or not the young person receives a wage for his or her work) is in:
  - the collection or delivery of goods including loading and unloading;

- carrying or running errands either outside the business premises on which they are employed, or in a club or hotel, in connection with the newspaper business, or at a place of public entertainment (including public and Turkish baths!);
- operating lifts;
- operating cinematographic equipment;
- receiving or despatching goods at a laundry, dye or cleaning works or other factory;
- premises in which intoxicating liquor may be sold after 11pm (excluding canteens);
- retail trade carried on in a residential hotel or theatre.

The restrictions under the Young Person's Employment Act 1938 are:

- an overtime limit of 6 hours in any week or 50 hours in any year, with 12 as the maximum number of weeks in any year in which overtime may be worked;
- no nightwork between the hours of 10pm and 6am. The young person, in every 24-hour period from mid-day to mid-day, must have a rest of at least 11 consecutive hours which must include 10pm to 6am;
- a maximum of 5½ days' employment in every 7 days. On at least one weekday (including Saturday) you must release young people no later than 1pm; if they work on a Sunday, they must have a day off in lieu in the week immediately preceding or following;
- there must be a rest period after 5 hours of work. This must be at least ½-hour, and ¾-hour if working hours include the period between 11.30am and 2.30pm.

Not only must you follow all these restrictions but you must also keep records identifying young employees by name, giving their ages, hours worked, meal and rest intervals and overtime.

Employing young persons in a factory
Under the Employment Medical Advisory Service Act 1972, if you take on young persons you must notify the local careers office. You must also observe the limits on employment hours, which are shown on the following page. Sunday working in a factory by young people is generally prohibited.

Overtime. There is a limit of 6 hours per week and 100 hours per year, to be spread over not more than 25 weeks.

Shiftworking. Night shifts are forbidden to young people but the Health and Safety Executive may give dispensation for day shifts beginning at 6am and ending at 10pm, and for the hours of 6am to 2pm on Saturdays. However, young people must have a continuous spell of 11 hours' rest between shifts.

	5-day working	6-day working
Maximum daily period on site	12 hours (Mon-Fri)	weekday: 11 hours Saturday: 6 hours
Maximum daily hours worked (excluding breaks)	10 hours	9 hours
Maximum weekly hours (excluding breaks)	48 hours	48 hours
Maximum continuous spell	4½ hours (5 hours if a 10-minute break is allowed)	4½ hours
Earliest starting time	7am	
Latest finishing time	weekdays: 8pm Saturday: 1pm	

Holidays. Some are mandatory for young workers, ie Christmas Day, Good Friday and bank holidays and at least half any other holiday entitlements must be permitted between 15 March and 1 October.

You must keep records of all young people employed, together with date of birth and employment details. It is an offence not to keep such a register.

You must also display a notice, form F11, specifying the period of employment for each day of the week and the meal intervals for each person.

Forbidden employment. You may not employ under-18s in betting shops or bars or in any other betting transactions, and employment in certain lead processes are also banned.

If you employ many young people, you should watch the progress of the Employment Bill carefully.

Employing EC nationals

The Treaty of Rome contains the basic right for nationals of countries which are signatories to the Treaty to move freely between member states of employment. The Treaty of Rome provides that:

> freedom of movement (for workers) shall entail the abolition of any discrimination based on nationality between workers of the member states as regards employment, remuneration and other conditions of work and employment

with the exception of public service (which includes the police but not local authorities).

This means that Belgians, Danes, Germans, French, Irish, Italians, those from Luxembourg and the Netherlands, and Greeks can come and work in the UK without a work permit. The Spanish and Portuguese will be able to do so once they have served their seven-year qualifying period to become full member states.

Employing Commonwealth citizens

Commonwealth citizens who can prove that one of their grandparents was born in the UK can come and work here for a period of 12 months without a work permit. Otherwise Commonwealth citizens are treated like any other foreign (non-EC) national.

Employing foreign (non-EC) nationals

If you want to bring in employees from overseas (including Americans) they must have a work permit. It is your responsibility to obtain this for a named worker before he or she enters the country. Work permits will only be issued if:

- a genuine vacancy exists;
- the vacancy requires professional qualifications or other expertise (eg highly qualified technician, French trained chef);
- there are no UK candidates and you have made genuine

efforts to find someone, including notifying the PER and advertising nationally and in the EC;
- the application is for a named worker for a specific job with a specific employer;
- the wages and conditions of employment are not less favourable than those to be found locally for similar work.

You should apply for a work permit at least eight weeks before it is needed. Permits are normally for 12 months in the first instance. If a permit holder wishes to change his job, he must have the approval of the Department of Employment. After four years he can apply for permanent settlement, the time limit on his stay can be removed, and he is free to take up any employment without reference to the Department of Employment.

If you employ someone who should have a work permit and does not, or who has changed employment (perhaps to join you) without Department of Employment approval, and this is discovered, that person risks deportation. There appear to be no penalties for the employer.

Employing disabled persons

The Disabled Persons (Employment) Acts 1944 and 1958 place certain obligations on employers, the main one of which is that if you employ 20 or more people, you should fill a quota of that number with registered disabled people. The standard quota is 3 per cent. While it is not an offence to be below that quota, you have a duty to engage registered disabled persons when vacancies arise and must not employ anyone else without a permit from the local Jobcentre. You must also keep records of those registered disabled people whom you employ, how many people you have employed under a permit, and whether or not you have any employees in designated employment. ('Designated employment' is employment of registered disabled people in occupations reserved for them, ie car park attendants and electric passenger lift attendants. People employed in these occupations do not count towards your quota.) The MSC (now the Training Agency) published a voluntary code of practice in 1984 entitled 'The Employment of Disabled People', which sets out guidelines for employers.

Employing people with a criminal record

People who have had a long custodial sentence will normally be helped to find employment by one of the agencies dealing with ex-offenders. You are free to choose whether or not you wish to employ such people.

There is, however, an Act called the Rehabilitation of Offenders Act 1974, which says that if a person has been convicted of certain offences and then had a period free of convictions, he or she is deemed to be rehabilitated. You must not take that previous conviction into account in deciding whether or not to offer a job to such a person. The Act applies only to probation or custodial sentences of not more than 30 months. Some professional people such as accountants can never be deemed to be rehabilitated, and those in contact with young people under 18 must also disclose any offences if requested (Rehabilitation of Offenders Act (Exceptions) (Amendment) Order 1986). The periods of rehabilitation are shown below.

Sentence	Rehabilitation period
A sentence of imprisonment or corrective training for a term exceeding 6 months but not exceeding 30 months	10 years
A sentence of cashiering, discharge with ignominy or dismissal with disgrace from Her Majesty's service	10 years
A sentence of imprisonment for a term not exceeding 6 months	7 years
A sentence of dismissal from Her Majesty's service	7 years
Any sentence or detention in respect of a conviction in service disciplinary proceedings	5 years
A fine or any other sentence subject to rehabilitation under the Act	5 years

Making a job offer

Once you have selected your chosen candidate, it is important to make a job offer as soon as possible. If you delay for too long you may lose him or her. You may wish to make the offer conditional on a satisfactory medical examination and the receipt of satisfactory references. Whatever the level of the post, it is sensible to take up references yourself once the candidate has given you permission to approach the referees. It is usually better to talk directly to those providing a reference because you can learn more about the candidate and his or her strengths and weaknesses in a conversation than from a letter. So that you are seen to be genuine, it can help to write to the referee enclosing a copy of the job specification, and stating that you will telephone on a certain day to discuss the candidate. It is generally unreasonable to talk to a person's present employer until you have his or her permission. Some employers have been known to dismiss employees who are found to be job seeking.

Those whom you approach for a reference have no legal obligation to provide one. However, once they have agreed to do so, the information they give should be accurate. If a reference is given which is false in material facts, the people providing it may be liable for an action to be taken against them for defamation, deceit or negligent misstatement. In particular, spent convictions under the Rehabilitation of Offenders Act must not be disclosed.

While it is generally assumed that references are confidential, it is possible that they may be seen at some later date by the candidate, either because you set up a computerised personnel record system and he or she has rights of access under the Data Protection Act 1984, or because you have an open policy and allow employees access to their personnel files, or because you are ordered to reveal a reference by an industrial tribunal. This could apply particularly where you withdraw an offer of employment. This potential lack of confidentiality is one reason why many employers prefer to talk on the telephone when the employee poses problems. It is important that you should keep an accurate note of what was discussed in the telephone conversation.

Medical examination
There are a number of reasons why a medical examination before confirmation of a job offer is sensible:

- There may be some doubt about the health or stamina of candidates which have been identified through the interview process. It is better to clarify their actual state of health rather than reject them because of a vague worry. It is also kinder to candidates, because if the fears turn out to be justified the sickness benefit they may enjoy with the current, established employer will almost certainly exceed anything you would wish to pay new employees and their security of tenure is likely to be higher.
- Should potential employees be going to work on a process which is dangerous, with chemicals which can provoke allergic reactions, where physical stamina is essential, or where there are regulations laid down (eg lead processing) then a pre-employment medical can help in eliminating those who should not be asked to work in such an environment.

Writing the offer letter

Employees are entitled by law to be given written particulars of their terms and conditions of employment within 13 weeks of the commencement of employment. For this reason, the offer letter need not go into complete details about every aspect of employment with you but should outline the most critical features, ie those which might encourage a candidate to accept or reject a particular post.

If you have a standard document including all your terms and conditions, it can be useful to send this with the offer letter so that the candidate knows exactly what his rights and duties will be. If the offer letter itself is to be considered as evidence of terms and conditions, it should say so. The status of any accompanying company handbook should also be clear, whether for information or because some of it is contractually binding. As a minimum the offer letter should include;

- the job title;
- starting salary and salary review date;
- other benefits, eg company car, private medical insurance, pension;
- place of work;
- hours of work;
- comment that the offer is made subject to satisfactory references and medical examination;

- reference to any enclosed document with an indication of its status, ie part of contract, for information;
- reference to any other terms which might have been agreed at the interview stage, eg this year's holiday arrangements to be honoured, time off to be given to complete work for previous employer;
- an indication of when you would like the candidate to start and some reference as to how long the job offer will remain open.

The letter should summarise the terms on which you are prepared to offer employment. The candidate may of course, try to negotiate those terms. The degree of flexibility you allow will depend on how reasonable you believe the demands are in terms of the market-place, what agreeing to those demands would mean as far as other employees are concerned, and most importantly, whether you can afford it. It may also depend on how badly you want or need the candidate. If there are several others on the final shortlist who would do as well, obviously you are in a stronger bargaining position than if the candidate is the only likely person you have seen in months of searching.

Should you agree to modify your offer, make sure any arrangements are confirmed in writing.

The induction process

Before your new employee joins, you should work out a programme for his or her introduction to the company and fellow employees. If the firm is still few in numbers, it should be possible to introduce everyone by name and function on the first morning; otherwise plan introductions over the first few days, starting with those whose work will most closely impinge on that of the newcomer. Newcomers like to know as soon as possible who they will be working with, from whom their work comes and to whom it goes, so that they can put it into a logical context. It also helps to make sure that people know what you are producing or the services you are offering and how their job contributes to that. They also need to know the obvious things which are often overlooked:

- where all the facilities are – lavatories, cloakrooms, lockers, tea/coffee machines, canteen (if any) – and where wages are

collected and where to go if they have a problem;
- what the usual practice is about breaks, meal times etc. It can be comforting for a new employee to be 'looked after' by a longer serving member of staff for the first few days;
- where the first-aid equipment is and who is the first-aider;
- fire exits.

Record keeping

If you follow through the recommended procedures in this chapter, you can identify a number of forms and records which are useful in the recruitment process. The advantage of having your own standard documentation is that you can design it to suit your own needs and be confident that it covers all the information you want to convey or need to collect. Ensuring that you use the appropriate document will also help to promote logical and objective decision making. It is important, particularly as you begin to build your workforce, to steer between excessive bureaucracy and an ad hoc approach which makes it difficult to remember why you took the decisions you did about people.

As a minimum it is recommended that you develop the following systematic records. (Interestingly, none of these is a legal requirement.)

- defining jobs – a job specification form;
- determining the skills and attributes you are looking for in the successful candidate – an employee specification form;
- a standard layout for advertising – the local readers will begin to recognise you;
- a company application form – it provides standard information, relevant to the job, in a way in which many CVs do not;
- a record of applicants for a position, so you can be sure everyone is acknowledged and all except the successful candidate rejected;
- a brief interview summary (to remind you what each candidate's strengths and weaknesses were). It can be effective to invest in a polaroid camera and take a photograph of those who interest you;
- standard letters acknowledging applications, inviting for interview, turning down with or without an interview;
- an offer letter;

- request for references;
- outline induction programme.

With the wide use of wordprocessors it is much easier to make all letters individual and personal, maintaining a 'master' on file. Forms can be developed and maintained on a wordprocessor and kept up to date quite painlessly.

Summary

This chapter recommends a simple, logical and objective approach to recruiting staff:

- define the tasks which have to be done and create rounded, discrete jobs;
- identify the skills and attributes you need in the successful candidate;
- find suitable candidates by the most cost-effective methods;
- assess those candidates using methods which will allow you to identify the attributes you are seeking, eg intelligence tests;
- make a job offer to your preferred candidate, subject to medical check and references which you will take up;
- ensure your induction programme provides a proper welcome to your new employee;
- be aware of the need not to discriminate on grounds of sex, marital status or race at any stage of the selection procedure.

2
Contracts of Employment

Entitlement

Once you have become an employer, you must provide your staff with written terms and conditions of employment within 13 weeks of the date on which they join you. Even within these 13 weeks your staff are protected by certain statutory rights, eg to a week's notice after one month's employment (see Chapter 3 for more details), and they will also be entitled to rely on any specific points you have made in your letter offering employment. It may be that you provided written details when you made the offer, in which case these are binding on you and your employees from the first day of employment.

Exclusions

The main group of employees who are not entitled to a written statement consists of those who work for you for less than 16 hours per week. However, if someone works for you for between 8 and 16 hours per week, and does so for five years, that person becomes entitled to be issued with written terms and conditions if you have not already provided them.

Should an employee leave you and come back within six months, on the same terms and conditions, you do not need to reissue written particulars by law although it might make good sense to do so.

Putting terms in writing

The importance of putting into writing the terms on which you are offering employment cannot be overstated. If you do not do so and there is disagreement between you and your staff about their terms of employment, an employee has the right to ask an industrial tribunal to decide what particulars should be included and make them the subject of an order which will have effect as if it had formed part of the written terms which you should have provided. To avoid the determination of the conditions on which you wish to offer employment being made by a third party, therefore, establish those terms as soon as possible, preferably before the individual accepts the offer so that it is made quite clear what is being agreed to.

Many small employers are reluctant to tie themselves or their staff down in what they see as legalistic jargon and red tape – unnecessary, they feel, where there is goodwill and mutual trust. Unfortunately, when terms of employment are being disputed, goodwill tends to disappear and it becomes one person's word against the other's. 'I didn't intend . . .' has no force at an industrial tribunal. To create and maintain good relationships at work, it is best to be open and agree the terms *before* there is dispute. It will be impossible afterwards – and this may be years later – to remember what was alleged to have been said on either side during the initial recruitment interview.

Definitions

The legal requirement is for you to provide written details of the terms and conditions of employment. These are not a 'contract' as is often understood by the word, and need not be signed by either party to be legally enforceable. Many employers and employees talk about the written terms as the 'contract' however, because although they may not be couched in legal language and may not be signed, they do to all intents and purposes constitute a contract, breach of which on either side might be grounds for dismissal or resignation (followed by a claim for constructive dismissal – see Chapter 7).

If you wish, you may make your written terms more formal and issue a contract which both you and your member of staff sign. (Even if you decide to issue written terms only, to avoid later disagreements it is wise to ask an employee to sign that he or she has received them.) There are a number of different types of contract, the most common being:

Open-ended contracts
These contracts, which apply to the majority of people in employment, are for an unspecified period of time and are terminable by either side giving notice in the matter described in

the contract, eg 'If you wish to leave the company, you must give one month's notice in writing to the Managing Director.' Unless notice is given by either side, the contract continues although the details may be amended from time to time (see page 50).

Fixed-term contracts

As the name implies, these contracts are for a certain period of time only and will automatically come to an end when the period expires. Such contracts can offer the employer more flexibility than taking on people on open-ended contracts and can be valuable when you know that your need for certain skills or numbers of people will naturally diminish. There are a number of important points to consider before issuing such contracts:

- Non-renewal of a fixed-term contract at its end is dismissal. This means that if the employee has the length of service (two years) he or she may make a claim for unfair dismissal.
- It is important to state in the contract the date on which employment will cease. If this cannot be done, the contract is not considered to be 'fixed term'.
- Even fixed-term contracts may contain clauses which allow their termination within the specified period – and it is particularly important to allow for your right to dismiss in cases of gross misconduct.
- Where a fixed-term contract is for more than one year, as long as the agreement is in writing and has the employee's written acceptance of the terms, it may contain a waiver by the employee in which he or she agrees not to make a claim for unfair dismissal when the contract comes to an end and is not renewed. If the contract is for a fixed term of two years or more and the terms again are in writing, as is the employee's acceptance, he or she may also waive the right to redundancy payment if the contract comes to an end and is not renewed.

Contracts for a particular purpose

These contracts are offered to a person who is engaged to carry out a specific task and whose employment will cease once that task is complete, eg 'You are offered employment for the purpose of designing and installing a new computer system for stock control.' The contract ends when this is done, but because it is impossible to put an actual date on the completion of the work (though you may have a good idea of when you would like it to be completed) is *not* a fixed-term contract. Again, it is important to state in writing at the beginning of the employment that the contract is a short-term arrangement which will cease when the task is completed, and get the employee's written acceptance of this.

Short-term contracts
It is possible to employ people on any basis you wish provided that they agree and you are not contravening any laws or Wages Council orders. A short-term contract of three months or less may have some attractions where the longer-term need for staff is uncertain, especially since those employed under such contracts have fewer rights than other employees. Particularly they have no right to:

- statutory sick pay;
- pay during suspension on medical grounds.

However, if you try to avoid your responsibilities in these areas by offering employment on a series of continuous short-term contracts, you will find that continuity, in the eyes of the law, confers obligations upon you and the employment is deemed to be continuous.

Service agreements
These are usually offered to senior members of the company only, and often only to directors. They are often a mixture of an open-ended contract and a fixed-term contract, eg 'You are appointed Sales and Marketing Director for a period of two years after which employment will be terminable by six months' notice on either side', or may be a rolling fixed-term contract which, in effect, gives a guarantee of employment for the fixed-term period (eg two years) and which renews itself annually or within the life of the contract. Points to watch are:

- directors' contracts for a fixed-term period of more than five years must be agreed in advance by a meeting of the shareholders or they become null and void.
- Such contracts may seem to be a good way of locking in a key person for a critical period (part of the golden handcuff) but the obligation works both ways – should you wish to dispense with the services of someone who is protected by a service agreement, it can be expensive to 'buy out' the

remainder of the agreement.
- While some employees may welcome such an agreement as confirmation of their status, or the regard you have for their services, or both, others may be reluctant to commit themselves to an agreement which effectively hampers their freedom of action.

A contract for services

This is *not* a contract of employment and should not be confused with it. It is an agreement between you, the company, and a third party or parties, for the execution of work on your behalf (eg a contract cleaner, contract catering or security services). The people who carry out the work are not employees – they are either employees of the firm providing the service, or they are self-employed. This distinction can be important if the question of termination arises. The termination of a contract for services is usually a business arrangement, not a matter of an employer giving notice.

Complications arise where the person whose services are no longer required claims employee status. In determining this, if it gets as far as an industrial tribunal, the tribunal will look at such matters as: whether or not you paid the person directly and, if so, if he or she had PAYE and NIC deducted at source; who gave orders to the person concerning his or her work; how free the person was to come and go, work or not work etc. In other words, the tribunal will try to decide whether or not there was an employer/employee relationship (or 'master/servant' as the law puts it). Once more, this is an area where it is best to ensure that you and the person or persons concerned understand the basis on which they are carrying out work for you. If it is done through a third party, for example a security firm, there is usually no problem. Where you take on casual or temporary staff as and when you need them, pay them without deductions and accept that they may reject your offer from time to time, then a tribunal would probably determine that such people were self-employed. If, however, the tribunal's conclusion was that you were in effect in a 'master/servant' relationship, not only could you find yourself held to have unfairly dismissed such a person if your need for his or her services came to an end, but you might also find the Inland Revenue holding you responsible for the PAYE and NIC which should have been paid but had not been.

What must be included in a written statement

The law (the Employment Protection (Consolidation) Act 1978) lays down certain minimum details which must be included in every contract or written statement of terms and conditions of employment. Those details are:

(a) **Identification of the parties,** ie the name of the company (the employer) and the name of the employee. This is usually straightforward, but if you own several companies in a group it can be important to make it clear in the written document who the employer is – the company or the group.

(b) **The date when the employment began.**

(c) **The date on which the employee's period of continuous service began,** if this is different from (b) above. This might arise if a person transferred from one group company to another and all service was held to be continuous, or if you took over another company and its employees and service were deemed to be continuous from the time when the person joined the original employer.

(d) **The scale, rate or method of calculating remuneration** (including overtime pay, bonus payments etc), ie how much you are going to pay the person and how this amount is arrived at if it is not a straightforward weekly, monthly or annual amount but varies with hours, productivity etc. Where you intend to pay for overtime working you should indicate what the rate will be (eg time and a quarter during the week and Saturdays, time and a half for Sundays or public holidays). Where bonuses are paid, you should state how the amount is arrived at. If, as the employer, you want the ability to vary bonus or incentive payments, you must state that they will be subject to variation from time to time as you see fit. Failure to include in the written terms the right to effect changes will mean that you cannot make changes without the consent of the employees affected, and at times of crisis their interests and yours might not coincide and agreement might be difficult to achieve.

(e) **The intervals at which remuneration is paid,** ie how often the employee will be paid – weekly, monthly, annually etc.

(f) **Hours of work,** including any contractual obligation to work overtime. An employer does not have the right to insist that staff work overtime unless the contract provides for it. If you think overtime working is something you will need, it is best to put a clause into the written terms and conditions stating quite clearly that employees will be required to work overtime when necessary. If, for example, you expect maintenance engineers to work every Saturday morning on overtime, put this into the written terms from the beginning.

(g) **Holiday entitlement,** including entitlement to public holidays, holiday pay and the right to any accrued holiday pay on termination of employment. You may make whatever arrangements you wish with your employees as there is no legal entitlement to holidays, even public holidays, unless your staff are bank employees or 'young persons'. However, if you do not offer what other local employers offer, you may not find many people anxious to take up employment with you! It is important that you clarify what the holiday year is, how entitlement is accrued, whether holidays can be taken when an individual chooses or if there is an annual shut-down during which employees must take their holidays, what happens if a person gives notice, and what happens in cases of dismissal for gross misconduct.

(h) **Terms and conditions relating to sick leave and pay** or absence through injury. As an employer you must pay statutory sick pay (SSP) to those who are eligible (see Chapter 3) but there are no obligations to pay sick pay as part of the terms of employment as well unless you wish to do so. Many companies do offer 'occupational' sick pay after employees have worked for them for a certain period of time. Sometimes such privileges are restricted to 'staff' employees, but with the growing harmonisation of terms of employment for staff and 'manual' workers, this distinction is used less frequently.

(i) **Information relating to pensions and pension rights.** If you offer a pension scheme as part of the terms of employment (and you cannot insist that employees join your scheme following the Social Security Act 1986) then details, or an indication of where details can be found, should be given in the written terms. Access to occupational pension schemes must be the same for men as for women, though at the present time the age at which pensions are payable may differ. (Normal Retirement Age (NRA), however, must not differ – if a woman wishes to carry on working until she is 65, if that is the NRA for men in your company she must also be allowed to work until that age.) If you do not offer an occupational pension scheme, and employees remain contracted into the State scheme, this must be stated. There is no obligation to set up your own scheme.

(j) **The length of notice** which an employee is obliged to give and will receive if employment is to be terminated. Notice given by you cannot be less than the legal minimum (see Chapter 3) but may be more if you so wish. In deciding how much notice you want to be given, you have to consider how important the individual is to you, how long it will take you to replace him or her and what is reasonable to expect.

If you require an unreasonably long period of notice, eg three months from an accounts clerk, you may simply encourage a staff member to break his or her contract and walk out. Your remedies in this situation are rather limited. You might take the member of staff to court and claim damages arising from breach of contract, but unless you could prove actual loss you are unlikely to gain much.

If the employee goes to work for a rival in breach of an express or implied term of employment, you might be able to seek an injunction forbidding this until the proper period of notice has expired. In reality, however, there is little you can do, and action arising from breach of contract will only sour relationships which may have been good up to that point. It is more sensible then to set periods of notice which are in line with other employers – one week for hourly or weekly paid employees, one month for clerical and junior management staff and three months for senior management and perhaps some specialists who will be difficult to replace.

In thinking about the length of notice you wish to give, the same considerations have to be taken into account. An important point to remember is that if you want to terminate employment lawfully, this has to be done within the terms of the contract. Thus, should the person prove unsatisfactory on day 2, and the notice you agree to give from the first day of employment is three months, you are *legally obliged* to give three months' notice, which is expensive. You may offer pay in lieu of notice but the employee's right is to notice, not payment in lieu thereof. (It is unwise to put into the written terms that you retain the option to pay money in lieu of notice as this then removes from such pay one of the main advantages to the employee, namely that it is usually free of tax. The Inland Revenue takes the view that if such payment is a contractual right, rather than an ex gratia payment made after employment has ceased, it is remuneration payable under the contract and therefore taxable.)

(k) **The title of the job** which the employee is employed to do. This is very important because the employee must obey 'lawful' orders from his employer, and in order for these to be 'lawful' they must be orders which can reasonably be said to relate to the work which the employee is employed to do. As there is no legal requirement to provide job descriptions, the main indication of the kind of work which is being offered is the job title.

Where you expect some flexibility from staff it is best to make this clear from the beginning, certainly emphasising this in the interview. The job title should also reflect this, eg 'Accounts clerk', not 'Sales ledger clerk, customers A–G'. Although there is some evidence that skilled tradesmen are now prepared to be more flexible in the range of tasks they will undertake and allow others to do, if you are heavily dependent on such employees it is essential to clarify from the start what you will require of them; otherwise you may have demarcation disputes and arguments.

(l) **The disciplinary rules** (or where they may be found) which apply to the individual. These must include the person to whom an appeal can be made if the individual is unhappy with any disciplinary measure taken against him or her and the name of the person to whom a grievance may be taken. (The Employment Bill 1988 aims to remove two requirements for those employing fewer than 20 people to include disciplinary rules in their terms and conditions of employment. Nevertheless it remains sound common sense to have written disciplinary rules and procedures.)

These are the minimum provisions for a written statement. You are free to put in whatever other terms you feel would be reasonable given the nature of the company, the work and the level of the employee. Many companies have different written terms and conditions for different levels of employee.

Other provisions in the written terms and conditions

Unless a condition is specified in the written terms, you have no legal right to insist on employees conforming to your requirements. It is sensible, therefore, to think about the aspects of an employee's behaviour which are likely to cause concern and cover these in your own written terms and conditions. Points which you might think of including are:

(a) The right to ask an employee whose health gives cause for concern to undergo a *medical examination* (at the company's expense). If this point is not included you cannot insist on an independent medical opinion, even if the person concerned has been absent sick for considerable periods.

(b) The right to *lay employees off* when there is no work for them. Some industries are accustomed to the use of lay-offs, and some collective agreements (that is, agreements made between the employer and one or more trade unions on behalf of employees), allow for lay-off, usually with some pay for a period at least. However, if you are not sure of the practice in your industry, and do not recognise a trade union for the purposes of collective bargaining with which you have entered into such an agreement, then you have no right to lay off people without pay unless the contract gives you that right. Employees will be covered by the guarantee pay provisions of the Employment Protection (Consolidation) Act (see Chapter 3) for part of a lay-off.

The right to lay off has usually been used with hourly paid employees, but it might be worth including in the terms and conditions those clerical and supervisory staff whose work may depend on orders coming through to the shop floor. If the clause is not included in their terms you would have to give them due notice, often a month at least depending on their other terms and length of service, that you intended to lay them off with effect from a specified day. By the time that day comes, the need for lay-offs may well have receded.

(c) The right to introduce *short-time working*. The same considerations as in (b) apply. However, unless the contract, or a collective agreement which forms part of the individual contracts of employees, gives you the right to reduce the working week because of lack of work, and to reduce pay accordingly, you will not be able to do so lawfully unless you either get the agreement of your employees at the time or give them appropriate notice that you intend to introduce such action.

(d) The right to ask employees to *work from different locations*, either permanently or on a temporary basis (including overseas postings if that is likely) or to travel widely in the execution of their duties. Again, unless it is made clear to employees that you have the right to ask them to move from Milton Keynes to Glasgow, they will be within their rights to refuse and, if you no longer need them at Milton Keynes, to claim a redundancy payment. If mobility is likely to become important, make sure you have the right to ask people to move.

(e) The steps you require employees to take if they are *absent through illness* or for other reasons. SSP has certain rules which employees must understand if they are eligible for payment through this scheme, but you may set other rules if you so wish which must be followed if employees are to be paid occupational sick pay. Under the SSP rules for instance, you cannot require an employee to notify you of absence through ill health before the end of the first working day of absence. Your own rules might ask for notification by 10am. If you are offering occupational sick pay you are free to make your own rules, but it is administratively inconvenient to make them too different from those relating to SSP.

SSP is payable only from the fourth qualifying day of absence. If you pay occupational sick pay, you may pay for all days absent sick until entitlement is exhausted or you might wish to set a limit on the number of casual days' absence which will be paid – perhaps no more than six in any twelve months – or you might do as SSP does and not pay for the first three days in any one period of absence. The choice is yours, but the terms and conditions should make clear to employees what their rights are.

(f) *The date of retirement.* This can be fixed by the terms of employment. Particularly where, for the company, this will differ from the State pension age (65 for men and 60 for women) it is essential that the retirement date is clearly laid out. You may fix retirement at any age you choose for your company, bearing in mind that 55 is usually the lowest age at which employees can become pensionable. However, although you may provide pensions at different ages for men and women, as stated above, you may not insist that women retire before men. Some companies have a common retiring age of 63 and some of 65, yet others allow women to retire at 60 if they so wish while requiring men to work to 65. The choice is yours – so is the willingness to allow employees to carry on working beyond whatever is normal retirement age for the company. If you are setting an early retirement age, employees should have adequate warning to allow them to make proper pension provisions.

(g) *The right to search employees or their property.* There is no automatic right of search, so if you feel this is likely to be important (if for instance you are manufacturing small, expensive consumer products such as watches or pens, or you have a retail or food outlet) it must be written into the terms of employment. Even where the right exists it is important to exercise it sensibly, eg women to search women, so that you do not face complaints of harassment. It is also important not to pick on one group or sex to search, and to remember to include the right to search managers' cars as well as those of others.

(h) *The protection of confidential information.* This falls into two parts: first, your (not unreasonable) expectation that employees protect your trade secrets while they are working for you – the written terms might include a clause to the effect that failure to maintain confidentiality will be regarded as gross misconduct – and second, the need to restrain employees from making use of information gained at the time of employment once they have left your company; this is known as restraint of trade.

(i) *Restraint of trade provisions.* You might assume that it is a simple matter to stop an ex-employee from using information gained while working for you either to lure away your existing customers or to sell the acquired skills to a rival. However, in order to prevent either of these events, you must first put a clause in the written terms making it plain that information gained in the course of employment must not be used once the employee has left (it is usual to specify a period, perhaps six months); that no customers of the firm must be approached within a certain period of leaving the company (again six months is not unreasonable); and that employment with competitors locally, or in some cases nationally or internationally, is prohibited for a certain period after leaving your employment. Having done all this, if an ex-employee chooses not to take any notice of these restrictions, you will have to apply to the High Court for an injunction to stop him or her and the burden of proof is on you, ie you must be able to convince the Court that your restraints are necessary and reasonable.

(j) *Whether or not the employee's terms of employment may be varied as a result of a collective agreement* entered into on his or her behalf by an independent trade union which is recognised for the purposes of collective bargaining by the employer. If you recognise a trade union, and intend to agree terms and conditions with the union on a periodic basis, and you also intend that agreement to be binding on the employees represented by that union, then the individual terms and conditions of employment must make this clear. If they do not, you may be unable to enforce them should an employee dissent.

This list is by no means exhaustive, but it covers the main areas which you ought to think about in determining the terms and conditions on which you wish to offer employment.

Implied terms and conditions

Once you have offered employment on certain terms which

have been accepted you are bound by those terms, as is the employee. There are, however, certain implied terms of contract – terms which are not set out in writing – which both sides may be able to rely on should relationships deteriorate.

As an employer, you have a right to assume that your staff will abide by the terms of the contract, and will not take bribes to disclose your business to third parties or set up in rivalry themselves while continuing to work for you. There is in effect a *duty of fidelity* from an employee to his or her employer.

You are also entitled to assume that your employees will *exercise due care* in carrying out their tasks, and that if payment as a skilled worker, craftsperson, or banker is accepted, they actually do possess these skills. (You should of course do your best to verify their presence during the selection process.)

For their part, employees have the right to assume that you will not require them to do *anything which is unlawful* in the course of employment and also that if they are in a supervisory or management position, their actions in that capacity will be supported by you.

Custom and practice

As well as the detail set down in the written terms and the implied nature of the contract, there may also be terms which become contractual (whether written down or not) by virtue of custom and practice. These may be tasks usually performed by an employee but not part of his or her normal work which the employer may wish to confirm as part of the job, or they may be 'rights' established by long habit, eg five minutes for washing up time at the end of a shift – time which has been taken and never repudiated by management. There are no clear-cut rules for deciding when custom and practice become enshrined in the contract, and it is best not to rely on goodwill or management authority to enforce or remove those customs. The main point for employers to watch is that they do not allow precedents to develop which can then be claimed to be 'custom and practice' and thus part of the contract.

Varying the terms of employment

The employer has no inherent right to change the terms and conditions of employment unless the written terms themselves give him the right, eg to lay people off or require them to move.

Changes to the contract need the consent of the employee, who may lawfully refuse to accept changes which he or she regards as detrimental.

Where changes are allowed for in the contract, the employer must provide written details of such changes within one month of their effect.

Summary

This chapter sets out the main considerations in putting the terms and conditions of employment into writing, and the legal minimum which such statements must contain. It also points out some of the other aspects of a contract which an employer might wish to include. An example of written terms and conditions of employment follows.

Specimen contract for clerical and administrative staff

This contract sets out the main particulars of the terms and conditions of employment between:

(Name of company): _____

and

(Name of employee): _____

Date on which employment commences: _____

Job Title: _____

Normal hours of work:
Official hours are 35 per week, Monday to Friday, but employees are expected to be co-operative in working outside these hours if necessary. Overtime is not paid.

Pay:
£ _____
This is payable in 12 equal monthly instalments by credit transfer on the last working day of the month.

Holiday entitlement:
The holiday year runs from January to December. Employees joining the company accrue paid holiday entitlement at the rate of 1⅔ days per month. In a full year the paid holiday entitlement is 20 days plus public holidays. Holidays must be agreed with your manager as early as possible, and at least one month in advance. Management will normally try to

accommodate individual preferences for holiday dates but the needs of the business may have to take precedence, particularly where inadequate notice is given.

Unused holiday cannot be carried over from one year to the next.

On termination of employment, holiday pay entitlement will be calculated to the nearest full month worked. If an employee has already taken holiday which has not been worked for, any excess holiday paid for will be deducted from the final salary.

Absence from work:
If you are unable to come to work for any reason, you must inform the company by 10am on the first day of absence. Failure to do so may render you subject to disciplinary action and may also bar you from company sick pay. In notifying the company you should indicate the reason for your absence and its likely duration.

Absence through sickness

Medical certificates:
All days of absence through sickness must be covered by a medical certificate. For the first seven days, a company self-certificate will be acceptable. For illnesses of more than seven days a doctor's certificate must also be produced on the eighth day, and weekly thereafter. Certificates should be sent to the Office Manager.

If your absence through illness lasts for less than a working week, you should complete a self-certificate on return to work and hand it in to the Office Manager.

Should you realise that your sickness will last for more than the working week, you should contact the office and ask them to send a certificate to you at home which you should complete and return by post.

Because of the rules relating to the payment of statutory sick pay (details below) it is important that your certificates indicate actual days of sickness even if they are sometimes days on which you would not have worked anyway, eg weekends and public holidays.

Company sick pay:
Company sick pay will be at the discretion of management and will not be unreasonably withheld. To qualify, you must have had six weeks' service with the company and have complied with the requirements for notification of absence and the provision of medical certificates. Maximum entitlement in any 52-week period is:

Length of service	Paid sick leave
less than 1 month	SSP only
1 month to 2 years	1 month full pay
2 years to 5 years	2 months full pay
5 years to 10 years	3 months full pay
Over 10 years	4 months full pay / 2 months half pay

Any sick leave or extended sick leave taken in the preceding 12 months before the current period of absence will be deducted from the entitlement in the above table to indicate the level of sick leave or extended sick leave to which you may still be entitled.

Where the company makes payment in times of sickness, this includes any entitlement to statutory sick pay.

The company will not normally make payment for more than six individual days of absence in any twelve-month period.

While the company will normally be sympathetic to cases of genuine sickness, illness or accident, prolonged or persistent absence for these causes may be investigated through the disciplinary procedure. Where there is concern for an employee's health and ability to carry out his or her work, the company reserves the right to ask that employee to submit to an independent medical examination, the cost of which will be borne by the company.

Statutory sick pay (SSP):
This replaces the State sickness benefit for the first 28 weeks of absence through sickness in any one period. It is paid to the employee by the company on behalf of the State and is subject to PAYE tax and NI contribution.

Where you are entitled to company sick pay, this will include any entitlement to SSP.

Should you not be entitled to company sick pay, eg through lack of service, your entitlement to SSP depends on:

(a) the number of days of sickness – there is no entitlement for the first three qualifying days;
(b) your normal weekly earnings – SSP is earnings-related (the wages department will provide the current rates if you ask);
(c) proper notification to the company of your absence through sickness (which you must give before the end of the first qualifying day); and
(d) proper provision of medical certificates, that is a self-certificate for the first seven days of illness and a doctor's certificate thereafter.

Your qualifying days for SSP are those you normally work, ie Monday to Friday inclusive.

If SSP is not due, any sick pay given will take account of any State sickness benefit paid and married women (paying the small NI stamp) will be treated as if they are receiving State sickness benefit.

Maternity rights

Ante-natal care:
If you become pregnant, you are allowed time off with pay for ante-natal care. In order to exercise this right, you must bring evidence of an appointment with the ante-natal clinic and show it to your manager, except for the first visit when you may not have an appointment card.

Statutory maternity pay (SMP):
The amount of SMP to which you are entitled will depend on your length of service and your level of earnings. If you have been with the company for six months or more, all your maternity pay entitlement will be paid by the firm in accordance with the statutory provisions at that time. If you have less than six months' service, you may be entitled to a maternity allowance paid by the DSS and based on your earlier National Insurance contributions.

The amount of maternity pay is:

Service with the firm	Entitlement from the firm
0–6 months	nil*
6–24 months	18 weeks at the flat rate**
more than 24 months completed at the start of the 14th week before the expected week of confinement	earnings-related pay 90 per cent of current salary for 6 weeks, plus 12 weeks at the flat rate

* If you do not have service with the company but meet the contribution requirements you will be able to claim maternity allowance from the DSS.

** The flat rate increases annually. The wages department will give you the current level.

Maternity leave:
The law does not require you to leave work at any specific date before your baby is due. However, if you are eligible for SMP, you are strongly advised to leave work at least six weeks before the baby is due. Should you work for any week, or part of a week, within six weeks of the date on which you expect your baby you will, by law, forfeit your right to SMP.

You may leave work 11 weeks before the baby is born and receive SMP from that time, if eligible. The remainder of the 18 weeks will be paid after the baby is born.

Returning to work after the baby is born:
Your right to return to work depends on your service with the firm and your observance of the correct notification procedure.

Service. You must have worked for the firm for two years before the 11th week before the expected week of confinement.

Length of maternity leave. Your maternity leave continues, if you so wish, to the 29th week after the week of confinement and may begin at the 11th week before the expected week of confinement.

Notifying the firm. The following procedure is necessary:

(a) You must produce a medical certificate stating the expected date of confinement and tell the firm that you wish to take maternity leave. This should be done as early as possible in your pregnancy.
(b) Three weeks before taking maternity leave you must inform the firm in writing that you intend to take it.
(c) The firm will write to you 49 days after the baby is born, seeking confirmation that you do intend to return. You must reply to that letter within 14 days or you lose the right to return.
(d) 21 days before you intend to return, you must let the firm know in writing. If you fail to do this the firm is entitled to refuse to allow you to return.
(e) You must return to work by the end of the 29th week after the actual date of confinement.

The job to which you return. This will be the same job you left, or one similar to it, with the same terms and conditions of employment which you enjoyed before your maternity leave.

Pensions:
Employees are contracted into the Government pension scheme.

Exclusive employment:
Employees are not permitted to take second jobs, eg in the evening, without written company agreement. Any person in breach of this requirement will be subject to disciplinary procedure and may be dismissed.

Termination of employment:
If you wish to terminate your employment with the company, you are required to give four weeks' notice.

Should the company wish to terminate your employment, for reasons other than gross misconduct, you will be entitled to notice as follows:

up to 2 years service	4 weeks
2–6 years service	6 weeks

Thereafter, an extra week's notice will be given for each full year of service up to 12 weeks' notice after 12 years' service.

Disciplinary procedure:
A copy of the company's disciplinary procedure is attached to this contract as Appendix 1 and employees are asked to read it carefully.

Grievance procedure:
If you have any grievance relating to your employment you should raise it orally with your manager. If the matter is not resolved within seven working days, you may raise it in writing with . . . who will make a decision about the matter within the following seven working days.

Health and safety at work:
Employees are reminded that they have a statutory duty to observe all health and safety rules and take all reasonable care to promote the health and safety at work of themselves and their fellow employees. Wilful breaches of the health and safety policy will be dealt with through the disciplinary procedure.

Signed on behalf of the Company:

_____

Name:

Job Title: Date: _____

I agree to the terms and conditions of this contract, and acknowledge that I have received a copy.

_____

(Employee's name)   Date: _____

The firm's disciplinary procedure

The main aim of the firm's disciplinary procedure is to help an individual to improve his or her performance, conduct or attitudes where these are giving cause for concern. Employees will be given opportunities to effect the necessary improvements. Ultimately, however, if the disciplinary procedure does not have the desired effect it will culminate in dismissal. The normal disciplinary procedure is in three stages.

Stage one: a verbal warning
Where an employee's performance, conduct or attitudes are giving rise for concern, and informal proceedings have not been effective, the employee will be interviewed by his or her manager and be told of the reasons for the interview and why the firm is unhappy about performance etc. Improvements will be agreed and a time scale by which they should be effected. A note of the interview will be put on the employee's record together with the agreed course of action. It will be made clear to the employee that this is a formal, though unwritten warning and that it does form stage one of the disciplinary procedure.

Stage two: first written warning
Should the improvements agreed in stage one not take place, the employee will be interviewed again by his or her manager. This time the requirements will be spelt out in writing and the employee reminded that

this is the second stage of the disciplinary procedure. A copy of the letter goes on the employee's file.

Stage three: second and final written warning
Should improvements still not have happened, the employee will be interviewed again and the requirements spelt out again in writing. This time the employee will be warned that failure to reach and maintain the standards required will lead to dismissal. Offences which merit a warning include:

1. Bad time-keeping.
2. Persistent absenteeism.
3. Accidental damage to the firm's property in the course of duty.
4. Quality, quantity or accuracy of work below accepted standards.
5. Any activity outside the scope of normal accepted employment practices.
6. An intentional act of racial or sex prejudice or discrimination.
7. Not complying with conditions of employment laid down by the Company.
8. Consumption of alcohol or taking of drugs on the premises.
9. Wilful non-compliance with health and safety rules.

This list is not intended to be exhaustive.

In some circumstances, if the offence is thought to be serious enough, it could warrant a written warning or a final written warning without the preliminary stages of the procedure.

Summary or instant dismissal
Some offences commonly called 'gross misconduct' are so serious that an employee who commits one of them becomes liable to dismissal without going through the full disciplinary procedure. In such circumstances the firm will investigate the facts of the matter; if after hearing the employee's case, the firm determines that dismissal is the right course of action, it reserves the right to dismiss the employee with no notice or payment in lieu of notice or holiday pay. If an employee has to be suspended from work during an investigation, such a suspension will be without pay unless the employee is subsequently reinstated. Examples of gross misconduct include.

1. Not complying with reasonable instructions from those in authority, given in the course of their duty.
2. (a) Proven theft.
   (b) Fraudulently appropriating the firm's monies.
   (c) Misleading the firm about sickness records or payment or about money received from the DSS or a claim against a third party.
3. Taking a second job without permission.
4. Calculated use of abusive language to another employee or superior.
5. Any form of negligence or recklessness leading to a loss by the firm.
6. Causing malicious damage to property belonging to the firm, to a client or to another employee of the firm or client.

7. Fighting with another employee while on the firm's premises or threatening to commit actual bodily harm to another employeer while on the firm's premises or those of a client.
8. Falsifying petty cash or other individual expenses for gain.
9. Creating problems with a client through abusive behaviour, misappropriating the client's assets or creating problems with his staff.

This list is not intended to be exhaustive.

Appeals against disciplinary action
Any employee wishing to appeal against disciplinary action may do so in writing to . . . who will respond within ten working days.

Health and safety at work policy

The promotion of health and safety measures is regarded as a mutual objective for management and employees at all levels. Therefore, Management will:

1. Provide and maintain safe and healthy working conditions in accordance with the relevant statutory requirement.
2. Provide integrated safety/job training for all employees where appropriate.
3. Provide all necessary safety devices and supervise their use by:
   (a) making regular office safety inspections;
   (b) stimulating joint consultation on safety matters.

Employees should respond to the above by:

1. Working safely and efficiently and by meeting statutory obligations.
2. Reporting incidents that have led or may lead to injury.
3. Adhering to company procedures for securing a safe workplace.
4. Co-operating in the investigation of accidents with the object of introducing measures to prevent a recurrence.

The three fundamental points of this policy are that:

1. The safety of employees, equipment, and the public are paramount;
2. Every effort will be made to reduce the possibility of accidents;
3. Safety will take precedence over expediency.

3
Statutory Rights in Employment

Chapter 2 looked at the details which you must or may choose to include in the written terms and conditions of employment. There are, however, other rights which employees have and which derive directly from the law. These need not be specified in the details which you provide, but you will still be bound to observe them should the situation arise. The most important are included in this chapter.

ELIGIBILITY

Generally speaking, the major statutory protections are given only to employees who usually work in Great Britain under a contract which requires 16 hours' work per week, or to those who have worked for 8 to 16 hours per week for the same employer for five years or more. Some of the rights can be exercised only after a specific period of service.

MAIN ENTITLEMENTS

Guarantee payments

These payments exist to provide employees who are laid off from work with some minimum protection. If the employer lays people off for a whole day or days they become entitled to receive £11.30 per day (as from 1 April 1988) for a maximum of five days in any period of three months. If you have already agreed contractual lay-off payments with your employees, perhaps as part of a negotiated agreement with the union, then the Secretary of State may exempt you from these requirements (as long as your own agreement is at least as generous as the statutory requirement). This particular benefit is of most use to manual workers who are often, by custom and practice, laid off without pay. As an employer, you should remember that unless the contract of employment with clerical, supervisory and management staff expressly allows you to lay such staff off without payment, you are not able to do so (see Chapter 2). Guarantee pay would not therefore come into effect. The amount of guarantee pay is usually increased annually, at or around 1 April. Employees with less than one month's continuous employment, or on a fixed-term contract of three months or less, are excluded.

Medical suspension pay

The Employment Protection (Consolidation) Act 1978 (EP(C)A) says, in Section 19 that if you suspend employees from work on medical grounds as a result of a statute, regulation or code under the Health and Safety at Work Act (1974) (HASAWA) which is listed in EP(C)A Schedule 1, they are entitled to full pay for 26 weeks and any dismissal during this period is unfair. However, no pay is due if such employees are actually bodily or mentally unfit for work or if they are provided with suitable alternative work, contractual or not or if they refuse to comply with your reasonable requirements to ensure that their services are available.

The medical suspension provisions apply in specified circumstances only, and these are set out in EP(C)A Schedule 1. They include regulations designed to protect those who work in paint and colour manufacturing, yarn dyeing by lead compounds, vitreous enamelling, tinning, lead smelting, indiarubber and chemicals and radioactive substances. Such industries or processes are normally the subject of particular regulations and often require regular medical checks.

If for instance you employ someone in an activity involving radioactive material and a routine check shows that his or her level of radioactivity is higher than the prescribed limits, then if there was no other work that person could do for you without being exposed to further risk, until that level has returned to what is considered acceptable, the employee is entitled to be suspended on full pay. Ironically, if he or she should fall ill with measles during the period of suspension, and you would not normally have paid sick pay, you would be entitled to withhold pay, apart from SSP, for the period of that illness.

If you cannot operate without someone in the job which your suspended employee would normally be doing, you can take on a replacement on a temporary arrangement and fairly dismiss him or her when your employee is fit enough to return to work.

Should you fail to make a payment to someone who is suspended in this manner, then he or she may take you to an industrial tribunal which can order payment.

Maternity rights

Ante-natal care
All pregnant employees, regardless of length of service, are entitled to time off for ante-natal care. You can require an employee to produce evidence of appointments at ante-natal clinics if you wish (except for the first visit). This time off is with pay at her hourly rate for the period of absence (Employment Act 1980, S13).

Again, if you refuse to pay or to allow time off, the employee may take you to an industrial tribunal.

Protection against dismissal when pregnant
To qualify for this right, employees need to have two years' continuous service. It is unfair to dismiss a woman wholly or mainly because she is pregnant.

However, if you can show that she is or will have become, by the date of termination, incapable of adequately doing the work she is employed to do or that her continued employment would be in breach of statutory duty, the dismissal will be fair. The burden of proof is on you, the employer, and some medical evidence will be necessary.

The dismissal may still be unfair if there was suitable alternative employment available and you did not offer it to her. This alternative employment, to be deemed 'suitable', must start immediately after the old job ends; the work must be such that it is both suitable for the employee and appropriate for her to do in the circumstances (ie, her pregnancy) and should be broadly similar and not substantially less favourable to her in terms than her previous contract.

Replacement staff may be engaged under EP(C)A S61. You have no right to determine when maternity leave should begin – you cannot for example insist on dismissal at the eleventh week before the expected date of confinement. The employee can choose to work so long as she is fit. However, if the employee now wishes to work for any part of the 'core' time when she is receiving statutory maternity pay, she forfeits her right to that payment, so this helps employers to encourage women to take adequate

Statutory Rights in Employment

maternity leave both before and after the baby is born (see 'Statutory maternity pay' below).

Statutory maternity pay

There are two levels of statutory maternity pay (SMP) and entitlement will depend on length of service. As the employer, you are responsible for making this payment to your employees and may claim it back as you do with statutory sick pay (see below). The two-tier payment consists of (a) an earnings related element payable for *six* weeks, and (b) a flat rate element for *twelve* weeks. Eligibility is illustrated below:

Service with current employer	Entitlement from employer
0–6 months	Nil*
6–24 months	18 weeks flat rate element
More than 24 months completed at the start of the 14th week before the expected week of confinement	The earnings-related element for 6 weeks plus the flat rate element for 12 weeks

* If your employee meets the contribution requirements, however, she will be able to claim maternity allowance from the DSS.

Amount of SMP
The flat rate element is paid at the same level as the lowest weekly rate of statutory sick pay (£34.25 as at April 1988 and revised annually). The earnings related element is 90 per cent of the employee's normal weekly wage. Both elements of SMP are subject to income tax and National Insurance contributions.

Earnings qualification
There is an earning qualification: if your employee's average earnings do not equal or exceed the lower earnings limit for National Insurance contributions over the past eight weeks before

SMP becomes payable, she is not eligible. Women who opt to pay the reduced rates of NI contributions are eligible for SMP (as for SSP) as long as they meet the earnings qualification.

Reclaiming SMP
You can reclaim money paid under SMP in the same way as you reclaim SSP – by making appropriate deductions from your tax and NI returns to the Inland Revenue.

Timing of leave
Most women will be eligible for 18 weeks' SMP, either flat rate or a combination of that and earnings related. While the rules for maternity leave as enacted in the EP(C)A have not changed, there is obviously scope for flexibility in the timing of departure from the company if the woman is not eligible for maternity leave or chooses not to return to work. There is now a concept of a 'core' period of 13 weeks, starting six weeks before the baby is due. This means that women are strongly encouraged to take at least six weeks' leave on either side of the birth, the encouragement coming from the loss of the flat rate of SMP for any part of that 13-week period which is worked. The other five weeks can be taken when the woman wishes, ie either before or after the birth.

The right to return to work
Those of your employees who have sufficient service are entitled to take maternity leave. To be eligible, they must have been employed by you for 16 hours a week or more (or for between 8 and 16 for five years or more) for two years before the date on which the baby is due. To exercise that right, an employee must then follow the rules set out below:

- She must state in writing that her absence is due wholly or mainly to pregnancy, that she intends to return to work, and the date of confinement or the expected week of confinement (EWC).
- You have the right to enquire of her after the 49th day following the EWC whether she intends to return. If she does not reply in writing within 14 days affirming her intention, her right to return is lost unless it was not reasonably practicable for her to reply.
- She must give you 21 days' notice in writing of her intention to return to work on a certain date. Failure to do so deprives

her of the right to return. The return must take place by the end of 29th week after the actual date of confinement unless you ask her to put off her return for up to four weeks or if she is ill and needs to extend her absence – though she can only do this on grounds of illness for four more weeks.

Upon return she has complete continuity of employment. She is entitled to return to the same job or to one which is similar in status, duties and terms and conditions of employment to her contractual job. She is not entitled to a job more suitable to her present domestic situation. The contract must be on the terms of seniority, pension and other contractual as well as statutory rights which would have applied had she not been absent.

Should matters have changed in her absence, and there is no longer a job for her and there is a genuine redundancy (and any replacement engaged is discounted in determining if there is a redundancy) then she is entitled to redundancy pay, assessed on her continuous service and pay at the notified date of return. Such dismissals and the reasons for them are delayed until the notified date of return, and unfair dismissal and redundancy rights begin at that date. In addition to being redundant she will also be unfairly dismissed if you or an associated employer had suitable alternative employment which is not substantially less favourable to her than her previous employment and this was not offered to her.

Employees unfairly dismissed can, of course, ask for reinstatement or re-engagement.

If you employ fewer than five people (including any in associated companies who are treated as one employer) and you can show that it is not reasonably practicable for you to offer even alternative employment, you can refuse to take the woman back and the dismissal will then be fair.

Public duties

All employees are entitled to reasonable time off for public duties. In some cases it may be reasonable to expect the employee to use some of his or her own time to make up part of the lost work. If you refuse to allow time off, your employee can apply to an industrial tribunal which will make a declaration of his or her rights and award compensation. It cannot draw up clauses to cover time off and incorporate them in the contract. The public duties concerned are:

Justice of the Peace
Member of local authority
Member of a statutory tribunal
Member of a Health Authority
Governor of school (local or State) or maintained educational establishment
Member of a Water Authority or River Purification Board.

This time off is without pay (unless you wish to pay), and in deciding how much time off is reasonable you are allowed to consider the extent to which you depend on the person to carry out his or her job (it might be difficult to release a shift supervisor for example) and any other time off the person has, perhaps because he or she is a health and safety representative, a shop steward etc.

Rights in insolvency

Should you, as an employer, become insolvent, some debts to employees are protected. Insolvency is defined as occurring either when a person:

- becomes bankrupt,
- makes an arrangement with creditors,
- has a receiving order made against him, or
- has died and his estates are being administered under the Bankruptcy Act 1914;

or when a company

- has a winding up order against it,
- resolves to be wound up voluntarily,
- has debenture holders exercise their rights against property subject to a floating charge.

The rights which are protected are:

- up to eight weeks' back pay,
- payment for the statutory notice period,
- up to six weeks' holiday pay (accruing during the last 12 months),
- basic award of compensation,
- reasonable reimbursement of fee or premium paid by an articled clerk,

- guarantee pay,
- medical suspension pay,
- time off pay,
- protective awards.

Contributions by employer and employee into occupational pension schemes, ie payments which the employer should have made on his own behalf or has deducted from the employee's pay but not transferred to the fund, are similarly protected but this is limited to the previous 12 months and may not exceed 10 per cent of the wages due to the employee during those 12 months.

Transfer of undertakings regulations

If you decide to sell your company and you recognise an independent trade union, the union has to be informed and consulted. In addition, employees automatically become employees of the new employer as if their contracts were originally with him. The new employer takes over the employment liabilities of the old employer with the exception of criminal liabilities and occupational pension rights. Trade union consultation must include:

- when and why the transfer will take place;
- the legal, economic and social implications for affected employees;
- what action, if any, the employer intends to take in relation to affected employees;
- what action the new employer intends to take.

A dismissal arising out of the transfer of a business will be automatically unfair unless the employer can show the reason was for an 'economic, technical or organisational reason entailing changes in the workforce'. Even if there is such a reason the dismissal must still satisfy the 'reasonableness' test. Transfers where these regulations apply include,

- when the whole or part of a sole trader's business, or a partnership, is sold as a going concern;
- where two companies cease to exist and combine to form a third;
- where a company, or part of its business, is bought by

another, provided this is done by the second company purchasing the assets and the business (and not the shares only) of the company being transferred.

If there are special circumstances which make it impracticable for you to fulfil the information or consultation requirement, you must take whatever steps as are 'reasonably practicable' in the circumstances.

Complaints by employees claiming unfair dismissal, or by trade unions because you have not complied with the information or consultation requirements, may be made to an industrial tribunal.

Equal pay

Men and women should be paid the same for doing the same jobs, jobs which are broadly similar, jobs which have been rated as equal through a job evaluation exercise, or which are deemed to be of equal value. If you are not paying equal pay, the woman or man concerned may make a claim to an industrial tribunal comparing her or his job with that of the person (who must be of the opposite sex) with whom he or she claims equal pay. The only defences open to the employer are either to prove that the jobs do not fall into the categories listed above, or that the variation in pay is due to a 'material difference' (other than the difference of sex) between the two cases. The procedure for a claim for equal pay goes like this:

(a) The employee makes an application to a tribunal for equal pay. He or she may choose the person with whom he or she wishes to be compared.
(b) The matter is referred to a Conciliation Officer. If it is not settled here, it is referred on to
(c) A tribunal hearing. There is
(d) An initial enquiry by the tribunal to see if parties would like an adjournment to reach a settlement.
(e) The tribunal will determine if the case is:
– same work,
– similar work, or if
– there is an existing job evaluation scheme.
(f) If a job evaluation scheme exists, the employee can raise the question of bias in the system.
(g) If the work is not the same or similar or there is no job

evaluation scheme (or a biased scheme) and the comparison which is being made is not ludicrous, then the industrial tribunal must appoint an 'independent expert' to undertake a job evaluation. (Experts have been appointed to a panel by ACAS which is not responsible for their decisions.) The expert is instructed to report on the question referred.
(h) The expert can collect information and copies of documents from both parties and others. He has no legal power to inspect the work. He cannot get information from the Conciliation Officer. He must take into account representations made to him.
(i) Before drawing up his report he must communicate his findings in writing to the parties and summarise their representations in his report.
(j) The report must include reasons, representations and conclusions. It must be made within six weeks. After 42 days the parties or tribunal can ask the expert the reason for the delay and the case may be transferred to another expert. Copies are sent to both parties.
(k) The tribunal receives the report and can reject it on procedural grounds but cannot reject it because it disagrees with the result unless the result could not have been reached on the facts available.
(l) The parties and tribunal can ask the expert to explain his report and each party can field an expert.
(m) Facts found by the expert cannot be questioned unless one party has refused to provide the information requested by the expert or the defence of material factor has been raised and on that issue alone new facts may be introduced.

Types of evaluation
Both under the Equal Pay Act and the Equal Pay Regulations the legislation refers to evaluation systems which measure 'demands made on her' (for instance under such headings as effort, skill and decision) so it looks as though factor comparisons are essential. For more details about job evaluation techniques, see Chapter 4.

Back pay
Back pay can be awarded for two years but not earlier than 1 January 1984 under the Equal Pay Regulations.

Statutory sick pay

As an employer, you must pay statutory sick pay to employees who qualify for payment. To understand the rules, you need to know the meaning of the terms currently used in association with SSP. The most common are:

period of incapacity for work (PIW). This is a period of absence from work for reasons of personal ill health, sickness or injury, and must be for four days or more.

qualifying days. The only days for which SSP is payable are 'qualifying days', ie those days on which the employee would normally have been expected to work. For office staff, this will usually be Monday to Friday; in retail it might be all seven days; if there is compulsory overtime on Saturday mornings for some staff, six days might be qualifying days. The important thing is to make sure that the qualifying days match normal working days. Those days which you intend to declare as qualifying days must be identified and your employees made aware of which they will be. This must be done in advance of any possible claims for SSP.

waiting days. The first three qualifying days in any period of absence do not attract SSP (unless they are linked to another PIW – see below). Therefore unless you pay occupational sick pay in accordance with your terms and conditions of work, these first three 'waiting days' are unpaid.

period of entitlement. To be eligible, a person must not have exhausted his period of entitlement. This is a period of 28 weeks in any PIW. This means a maximum liability of 28 times the appropriate weekly rate of SSP for each PIW. For other exclusions, see below.

linked periods. Some spells of sickness may be linked to other spells. This is said to be so when the gap between one PIW and the next is less than 8 weeks or 56 days. In practice this means that if your employee is ill for 10 working (qualifying) days, returns to work for four weeks and is then sick for a further 10 working days, this second period is 'linked' to the first and SSP will be payable for the whole period, ie there will not be another waiting period.

evidence of incapacity. This will normally be a self-certificate or a doctor's certificate. NHS certificates are not normally available during the first seven days of illness. The DHSS has the right to inspect records etc, and where you have paid or withheld SSP they may wish to see the evidence. It is important therefore to make sure that your employees understand the need to complete certificates and that you or your managers always ensure that this is done.

offset provisions. If you have a company sick pay scheme, any payment you make under that scheme may be offset against your liability for SSP.

Exclusions

Some employees are automatically excluded. These categories include:

- employees over pensionable age (65 for men and 60 for women) at the start of the period of incapacity for work:
- employees who are employed on a fixed-term contract of three months or less (three months equals 13 weeks);
- employees whose normal weekly earnings are below the lower earnings limit – at present £41.00 per week;
- employees who fall sick within 57 days of having claimed one or more of the following State benefits:
  - sickness
  - invalidity
  - non-contributory invalidity pension
  - maternity allowance
  - unemployment benefits following entitlement to invalidity pension.
- employees 'sick' on the date they are due to start their employment;
- employees 'workless' in consequence of a 'trade dispute' unless they can prove that they were not participating in, or had a direct interest in the dispute;
- employees who have not exhausted the same period of incapacity for work at the end of three years;
- pregnant employees for 18 weeks which begins with the eleventh week before the expected week of confinement;
- employees 'sick' outside EC countries;
- employees in prison or otherwise in legal custody; this does not include 'those voluntarily assisting police with their enquiries';
- mariners on foreign-going ships.

Note The above exclusions mean that there is no minimum service entitlement required to be eligible for SSP. All employees are eligible as long as they meet the lower earnings level.

How SSP works

If one of your employees is off work because of personal illness (absence to look after sick members of the family does not count), once the first three qualifying days have passed, SSP becomes payable as long as the person is entitled (ie he or she is not excluded) and proper notification of absence has been given. Under the SSP rules this need not be before the end of the first qualifying day. It makes sense to set up a simple system whereby employees know whom they should call, and that the person who receives the call notes that it has been made.

If it is clear that the employee is going to be absent for a week or so, he or she will need to complete a self-certification form. This you can design for yourself, but a model is given on page 51. Your own company rules about notifying sickness should say when you expect this self-certificate to be completed, eg while out sick and sent in, or on return to work. If the sickness lasts beyond seven days, the employee will need a doctor's medical certificate. You keep copies of all certificates as proof of your right to pay and reclaim SSP. The best place for storing these is either with the employee's personal file or with his or her wages details.

SSP entitlement should be calculated and paid at the same intervals as normal pay would be made. You must keep proper records. You can then reclaim SSP.

There are one or two more rules you should note:

- Employers may not contract out of paying SSP and any attempt to exclude, limit or modify an employee's entitlement to SSP or to require an employee to contribute to any costs of administering SSP is *void*. For example, the following practices are not acceptable:
  - requiring notification of absence before the minimum SSP requirements and, if this does not happen, causing the employee to lose entitlement to SSP;
  - making employees obtain private medical certificates at their own expense before paying out SSP.

  It certainly *does* mean that to dismiss an employee 'solely' or 'mainly' to avoid paying SSP will not avoid liability.

- Employers must pay SSP before the deduction of income tax. SSP is therefore classed as 'earnings'. NI contributions are paid by employers and employees.

Statutory Rights in Employment 71

- Employers are required to keep certain records for a minimum of three years after the tax year to which they relate and for each employee separately. These are:
  - dates of sickness absence of at least four consecutive days;
  - any days within such periods for which SSP was not paid, with reasons;
  - details of each employee's 'agreed working week' and/or qualifying days;
  - all SSP payments made, weekly, monthly and yearly amounts.

  For failure to keep records in the prescribed manner the employer may be fined up to £200 for any one offence and £20 a day for continuance of the offence.

- Employers are entitled to withhold payment of SSP where the employee does not give proper notification of his incapacity.

- If asked by employees, the employer must provide written statements of:
  - the days for which the employer considers himself liable to pay SSP;
  - the reasons why he has not paid for any other day for which the employee considers him liable;
  - amounts of SSP the employer accepts is owed.

  Questions arising about an employee's entitlement will be determined by an Insurance Officer who may refer the matter to a local National Insurance tribunal. There is also a further right of appeal to the Social Security Commissioner.

- In the event of the employer becoming insolvent, SSP is treated as a preferential debt.

- An employer must give a leaver's statement to a leaver who has a PIW (linked or unlinked) which is separated from the date the contract ends by eight weeks (56 calendar days) or less and where SSP was payable for one week or more. The statement must be issued no later than seven days after the contract ends. The new employer must take account of the weeks of SSP shown on this statement which may reduce his maximum liability towards the new employee in his period of incapacity for work.

Paying and recovering SSP

Paying SSP
SSP is payable by the employer for up to 28 weeks in any one period of incapacity for work. The weekly rates are flat rates and are payable to employees regardless of marital status and/or the number of dependants.

Daily payments of SSP are arrived at by dividing the appropriate weekly rate by the number of qualifying days in that week.

Employers will be expected to pay SSP on the first normal pay day after a period of incapacity has been formed. Payment may not be made in 'kind', ie benefits other than cash.

Average weekly earnings	Weekly rate of SSP
£79.50 or more	£49.20
£41.00 – £79.49	£34.85

(1988–89 figures)

Recovering SSP
All SSP payments properly paid to employees may be reclaimed by deducting the gross amount paid from the monthly National Insurance contributions paid over to the Inland Revenue. Where the amounts of SSP to be reclaimed exceed the amount of NI contributions to be paid, the balance may be recovered from PAYE payments to the Inland Revenue.

Employers are entitled to reclaim 107 per cent of SSP paid to compensate for the administrative burden. This figure is reviewed annually.

The role of the DHSS Inspector

DHSS Inspectors have the right to enter premises, inspect records, question people and require the production of documents. The purpose of the visit is to:

- check the records to see if you are dealing correctly with SSP;
- answer questions and advise about mistakes;
- instigate any other action the Department needs to take.

The inspectors will look at:

- agreed qualifying days
- application of linking rules
- application of waiting day rules
- the rate of SSP applicable
- the amount of SSP paid
- whether offset provisions have been applied
- the payment of SSP on correct days
- whether transfer and exception forms have been completed correctly and on time
- when self-certificates are required
- whether any individual has sent in four self-certificates in a 12-month period.

If you are contemplating dismissal of a sick employee it will obviously be more difficult to justify dismissal or prove frustration while entitlement is not exhausted. However, unless the contract provides otherwise, sick leave does not guarantee continued employment during this period. This point should be clarified in the contract, ie there is still a right to terminate while sick leave is not exhausted.

Finally, if employees are dismissed while absent through sickness, then they must be paid their wages, even if sickness pay has been exhausted, for the period of notice (EP(C)A S50 and Schedule 3). Any sick pay given to the employee will be taken into account. This does not apply if the employer has to give one week more than the statutory minimum period of notice fixed by EP(C)A S49.

Notification of absence for sickness

Employers are free to make whatever arrangements they wish, but should take into account that NHS certificates from a doctor are not available until the eighth day of absence. It is assumed that most companies have developed their own system of self-certification to cope with the first seven days of absence.

Relationship between SSP and occupational sick pay

Occupational sick pay is a matter for employers. They may pay what they like to whom they wish and may make whatever rules of eligibility that suit their businesses.

Statutory sick pay is payable under precise rules and regulations as outlined above and, as already described, employers may not 'opt out' of the system.

Accordingly, it is likely that the rules and regulations companies have determined as appropriate for their needs may differ considerably from those required under the statute. It is a matter for employers to consider whether some form of rationalisation is required between the two sets of schemes.

Those employers who continue to operate their sick pay scheme under different rules should be aware of some of the possible problems which may result in employees being entitled to SSP yet not company sick benefit, or vice versa. The most likely differences commonly found are:

Eligibility
Most companies require a service qualification for sick pay. SSP becomes payable without service qualification and from the start of employment. Remember also that SSP is excluded for some employees. Does the company scheme carry the same exclusion?

Length of entitlement and year
Company sick pay schemes operate on service years or calendar years. Length of entitlement is usually based on length of service – the longer the employment the longer the sick pay entitlement. SSP is based on the concept of a 'period of entitlement' of up to 28 weeks.

Waiting days
Few in-company sick pay schemes have waiting days. SSP has three for each period of incapacity except where there is less than an 8-week gap between illnesses.

Qualifying days
Most sick pay schemes work on the 'normal working week' basis. SSP may differ if other qualifying days are agreed.

Payment levels
Company sick pay is usually the 'gross' pay less the State benefit received and sometimes is reduced to proportional payments, ie half pay or quarter pay after fixed periods. Only if sick employees are paid *more* than the appropriate SSP rates can it be 'offset'. If at present fixed sums or percentages of earnings are paid or benefits received deducted, the company will need to look at the rates of company sick pay.

Holidays
Does the company sick pay scheme operate during annual holidays, or bank or public holidays? Under SSP these may be excluded or, if not, SSP may not be paid for holiday periods spent outside the EEC. If sickness during holidays is acknowledged for payment purposes the company's rules need looking at with SSP in mind.

Sickness – other than personal ailments
Many companies' schemes allow benefit for who are absent for reasons of family sickness, bereavements etc. SSP does not. It must be *personal* sickness to qualify.

General qualification rules
Most companies require 'evidence' of incapacity by notification on the first day, and provision of medical certificates on the third or fourth day (these now have to be private medical statements). Failure normally means no pay under the company scheme. Under SSP you cannot require notification earlier than the first qualifying day, or medical certificates before day 8 of the sickness.

Discipline
Failure to satisfy company sick pay scheme rules may lead to disqualification for pay and disciplinary action. You cannot stop SSP for disciplinary reasons.

The name DHSS (Department of Health and Social Security has been retained in this book, although the Department has now split into the Department of Social Security (DSS) and the Department of Health. The original term will probably remain in common use for some time.

4
Paying People

One of the fundamental principles of employment is that the employer rewards services provided by the employee by paying for them. If you fail to pay your employees you are in breach of contract. However, there is very little guidance for the employer about what he should pay. In setting up a payment system there are a number of factors which have to be taken into account:

- how much to pay,
- on what basis pay will be calculated,
- how often you will pay people,
- the form in which employees will be paid.

Deciding how much to pay

In most instances employers are free to pay what they choose. There are some exceptions:

- If your business falls within the scope of a Wages Council, there are minimum rates of pay and overtime pay which apply to employees over 21. The main Wages Councils still in existence cover:

    Aerated waters
    Boot and shoe repairing
    Clothing manufacturing
    Flax and hemp
    General and waste material reclamation
    Hairdressing undertakings
    Laundry
    Licensed non-residential establishments
    Licensed residential establishments and licensed restaurants

Made-up textiles
Retail bespoke tailoring
Retail food and allied trades
Retail trades (non food)
Sack and bag
Toy manufacturing
Unlicensed places of refreshment

- If you are a member of an employers' federation which negotiates on behalf of its members with trade unions representing employees, the negotiated settlement will set minimum wages and often other terms of employment as well. You will be expected to observe these minima which are often formalised in Joint Industrial Councils (JICs), National Joint Councils (NJCs), or Joint Consultative Councils.

In addition, workers in the agriculture industry have their minimum wages fixed by the Agricultural Wages Board.

The only bodies which can, under law, regulate wages are the Wages Councils and the Agricultural Wages Board. Both have inspectors who have the right to ask to see wages sheets, records of payment etc, and can institute civil proceedings on behalf of employees paid less than the minimum rate.

Other than amounts laid down by Wages Councils and the Agricultural Wages Board, there is no statutory minimum wage in the UK.

The two main factors which are likely to affect what you decide to pay are the relativities between different employees or groups of employees and the market rate.

Internal relativities

These should reflect the contribution made by different people. A foreman, for example, will expect to be paid more than the people he or she supervises, and a manager will look for an even higher level of remuneration. It is important to look at these relativities from top to bottom because payment at one end will have an impact at the other. For example, if the managing director is paid £15,000 and the other directors and senior managers around £10,000, this does not leave much scope for other levels of management or supervision, particularly if you employ skilled men whose annual wage without overtime may easily be around

£8,500. One way of deciding what the right relativities should be is to carry out a job evaluation exercise.

Job evaluation

As a company grows, it becomes important to formalise the 'felt fair' ranking on which differences in salaries and wages have been based. There are a number of ways of evaluating the worth of jobs to the company, and professional advice is available. Because of the implications of the 'Equal pay for work of equal value' regulations (see 'Equal pay', page 66), it is best to establish an analytical system from the start. This looks at jobs under a number of headings which can be chosen to reflect the company's processes but will almost certainly include skills, effort and decision making. If there is no job evaluation system or if one which is not analytical is being used, a company may find it difficult to rebut a claim for equal pay. A sound job evaluation system can be a great advantage to a company because as jobs change, or new skills are required, the mechanism for measuring their contributions objectively already exists and the new jobs can be slotted in without difficulty.

Market forces

While you are free (apart from the instances above) to pay what you like, unless your rates are in line with what other local or national companies are paying you will not be able to attract new staff or retain the ones you have. While for many people money is not the main motivator, nevertheless wages and salaries have to be adequate and considered to be a reasonable reward for effort expended if a company is to be able to recruit and retain the skills it needs. The same applies to benefits. Most managers, for instance, will now expect to participate in a pension scheme, have life and private health insurance and perhaps a company car. If, as a small employer, you do not want to offer this range of benefits, then to attract someone at a senior level there has to be some other inducement for them to join you. This may be either a higher salary or perhaps the promise of equity participation. A check on market rates can be made by carrying out your own survey, joining a local employers' group which exchanges such information, reading advertisements in the local and national press, and looking at national surveys or other statistics such as those published in the Department of Employment *Gazette*. General news items may report on findings from surveys as well.

Equal pay

Employers must not discriminate between men and women in pay or benefits given for the same job, jobs which have been rated as equal through a job evaluation system, or jobs which are held to be of equal value. The 'equal value' regulations mean that if, for example, a secretary believes her job to be of as much worth to the company as that of a skilled man who is paid more, she can make a claim against the company through an industrial tribunal. If the tribunal believes that she has reasonable grounds for proceeding with her claim, it will appoint an 'independent expert' to investigate and produce a report. The expert will in effect evaluate the jobs and come to some conclusions as to whether or not they could be deemed to be of equal value. The report is then admitted as evidence at a resumed industrial tribunal hearing. The tribunal will hear arguments from both sides and reach a conclusion. If the woman wins her case, the tribunal has the power to award back pay for up to two years.

Deciding the basis on which payment will be made

Thinking about 'how much' will give an indication of what you expect the weekly, monthly or annual earnings of employees to be. There is then a second set of decisions to be made – how is that sum going to be made up? For instance, most management and clerical salaries are quoted as annual sums, divided into 12 equal parts and paid at the same time each month. (The terms and conditions of employment must specify when and how the money will be paid.) Salaries are normally paid in arrears.

Wages for other employees are often quoted as an hourly or weekly rate (even though they may be paid monthly). The amount which is then due is the hourly rate multiplied by the number of hours worked. In both these examples, wages or salary due do not vary unless someone is unable to fill his or her contractual hours, eg through sickness. There are, however, some other considerations which should be thought about in setting up a salary structure:

- *Where earnings vary by time.* Consolidated time rate (CTR) is a substitute for the basic rate which is usually used in piecework to provide payment when no work is available or as a basis for overtime or holiday pay.
- *Payment for abnormal hours.* Examples are overtime,

shiftworking, unsocial hours, flexibility, stand-by or call-out payments.
- *Where earnings vary by quantity*. Illustrations include:

  - *piecework:* where pay varies with the amount which is produced and reward is based on a constant and specified price per unit or piece produced regardless of the time taken;
  - *payment by results:* a financial incentive for quantity;
  - *measured daywork:* payment is geared to an agreed level of output but is usually only withdrawn if it can be shown that failure to meet the target is the fault of the operators.

- *Bonus payments*. Should there be a fixed or basic element of pay and a variable one which depends for example on company profitability or performance? Possible forms of payment include:

  - *profit sharing:* this is usually paid as a bonus rather than forming the basis for a weekly wage, although an anticipated amount of bonus might well be included in any annual negotiations. It may be paid at any interval – weekly, monthly etc – but the employer will need good accounts to ensure that he is not paying out a share of profits which do not exist;
  - *added value:* 'added value' is the 'increase in market value resulting from an alteration in the form, location or availability of a product or service, excluding the cost of bought-out materials and services'. Some companies use added value measures as the basis for bonus payments. Again, these may be agreed in advance and form part of the annual pay settlement.

- *Profit-related pay (PRP)*. As well as the variations in pay listed above, there is also the government's Profit-Related Pay (PRP) scheme. This allows employers to set up payment systems in which part of the profit is paid to employees tax free. Unlike the illustrations above, PRP does have rules which must be followed if the tax benefits are to be obtained. More information can be obtained from the Profit-Related Pay Office, Inland Revenue, St Mungo's Road, Cumbernauld, Glasgow G67 1YZ.

- *Other elements in pay.* These may be either given as a one-off amount or consolidated into the basic rate. Such payments include merit awards, long service awards, time-keeping bonuses and service increments.

Further considerations

Spot rates versus salary bands? You may want to pay a specific rate for a job or put the job on salary bands. The latter method gives you some flexibility to reward employees with greater skills, ability, motivation etc.

Incremental scales or increases decided solely on merit? If you decide to use a salary band, will progression through the band be in automatic stages?

How often do you wish to review salaries and wages? Once a year is the most common; review does not automatically mean an increase.

If wages and salaries are to be increased, will an element apply to everybody as a 'cost of living' award or will all increases have to be earned through merit? If the latter, the company will need an accepted form of performance appraisal.

Although there is a variety of options, in most instances the basis on which companies pay tends to sort itself out fairly easily because industries have certain expectations, as do employees. It is, however, worth reviewing salary policies every two years or so to check that what was originally valid still holds true.

How and how often to pay

Since the Wages Act 1986 repealed the Truck Acts, employers have more flexibility in the way in which they pay new staff. (People who were employed by you before the 1986 Act and whose contracts allow them to be paid in cash must continue to be so paid unless they agree otherwise.) You may now make it a term of employment that staff, whatever their job, will be paid by cheque or credit transfer. There are both cost savings and security advantages to be enjoyed by using either method rather than payment by cash. Employees find it easier to make the transition to cashless pay if they receive their wages or salary at the same intervals as they received cash.

In determining pay intervals, the company should consider

- employee expectations,

- administrative convenience,
- cash flow.

Developing a philosophy

For employers, a payment system is a means to an end. It is one way of trying to match the aspirations of employees with the objectives of the company. The two are not always compatible but provide an opportunity for an open dialogue. As an employer you need to think about the extent to which you would like your payment system to:

- increase earnings,
- increase effort,
- improve quality,
- encourage flexibility,
- simplify negotiations,
- develop company loyalties,
- reward personal qualities,
- reflect company results,
- be competitive in the market-place,
- encourage promotion and self-development,
- give stable earnings,
- permit rapid changes in work organisation and technology,
- negotiate the impact of taxation etc.

If there is a conflict between the skills, attitudes and philosophy of the company and the requirements of the payment system, it will break down. This may happen if:

- the company is seeking a participative relationship with employees but has a payment system which is rigid, relies upon over-detailed controls, and leads to friction between work groups and supervision;
- the payment system which is introduced relies on co-operation and trust but management skills and attitudes cannot develop such a relationship.

Summary

There is very little legislation which constrains the way in which you pay people. You need to think about the objectives of your pay policy before you decide:

- how much,
- on what basis,
- when and by what means.

A salary structure should be designed to ensure that you can attract and retain the right calibre of employee who will work with you to achieve the aims of the company.

Checklist of PAYE forms

Forms for employers to fill in

P9D	Return of expenses payments for employees other than those for whom a P11D is appropriate	To be sent to to the Inspector by 6 May each year
P11 (87)	Deductions working sheet	This form or a substitute to be filled in every pay day
P11D	Return of expenses payments and benefits of directors and employees who earn at a rate of £8,500 or more a year including expenses and benefits	This form, or list if it has been approved by the Inland Revenue, to be sent to the Inspector by 6 May each year
P11Db	Form which confirms that all forms P11D, where needed, have been filled in and sent to the tax office	To be sent to the Inspector by 6 May each year
P13	Employer's permanent record of employee's details	You do not have to use this form but you may find it useful
P14	End-of-year return of pay, tax, National Insurance, SSP and SMP	This form or substitute to be sent to the Inspector by 19 April each year

P30Z **P30B(Z)**	Payslips for sending with payments to the Accounts Office	To be sent to the Accounts Office within 14 days of the end of each tax month
P34	For ordering forms	
P34(Z)	For use in Centre 1 only	This applies to Scotland only and refers to the computerised system in use there
P35 **P35(Z)**	Employer's annual statement declaration and certificate	
P35(MT)	Version of P35 for employers who send their returns on magnetic tape	
P35(CS)	Continuation sheet for P35	
P35(TAS)	Returns of awards under a Taxed Award scheme	
P38 **P38A**	Employer's supplementary returns with details of employees who were paid over £100 in total for the year but for whom a deductions working sheet was not completed or who were not entered on the P35	
P38(S)	For use when students are employed during the holidays where issued to the employer by his tax office	The student also has to complete the form
P39	Return of people who are employed by non-resident employers	Will be sent to employers who need to complete them

Paying People **85**

P45	For use when an employee leaves a job and when an employee starts a job	Available as separate forms or continuous stationery
P45W	Welsh version of notes on form P45 (part 2)	Avaliable on request
P46	For use when a new employee does not produce a P45	To be sent to the tax office or kept by the employer depending on the type of employee
P46(Z)	For use in Centre 1 only	
P46(car)	Advance details of a car and/or fuel provided for directors and employees who earn at the rate of £8,500 a year or more including expenses and benefits	
P47	Application for authority to make a refund of tax of more than £50 due on a new employee's first pay day	
P60	Certificate of pay and tax deductions	This form or a substitute be given to the employee at the end of the year. It is normally the third part of form P14 but there is also a version that is not part of P14 for employers who send end-of-year returns on magnetic tape
P61	End-of-year notification to an employee of tax refunds withheld during a trade dispute	
P62	End-of-year advice to an employee involved in a trade dispute	

P89(Z) Claim for allowances for superannuation contributions. For use in Centre 1 only

P160 Notification to the tax office of the retirement of an employee who is to be paid a pension by the employer — You can send a letter instead of using this form

P403 For use by firms paying holiday pay to employees

P440 Analysis of totals on P35 (TAS)

P440(CS) Continuation sheet for P440

P443 Certificate to employeee giving details of Taxed Incentive Award

TAS Payment Advice Advice note sent out with P35(TAS)

Forms for employees to fill in

P15 Coding claim

P28(S) Form to be completed by a student who is employed during his or her vacations. The employer also has to complete the form.

P46 Form for a new employee without a P45

Forms sent to employers

P6 Forms sent to employers by the tax office with coding or amended coding instructions. These are used throughout the year

P6(Z) Centre 1 version of this form

P7X	Instruction to an employer. Authority to amend suffix codes during the year when the government has increased personal allowances (eg at Budget time)
P9	A notice issued towards the end of one tax year with coding instructions for the next year
P9(Z)	Centre 1 version of this form

Code Lists replacing form P9, by arrangement with the tax office

P24	Covering form issued with code notifications on forms P9. These are sent to employers before the beginning of the tax year
P24(Z)	Centre 1 version of this form
P24N	Covering form sent to new employers
P35X	Notes to help you complete form P35
P46–5	A notice of a new or amended NI number
P48	Authority to refund tax to a new employee
P48(Z)	Centre 1 version of this form
P89A(Z)	Explanatory notes for form P89(Z)
P8	Deductions guide giving information about operating PAYE
480	Income tax: 'Notes on Expenses Payments and Benefits for Directors and Certain Employees'
P11D (guide)	A guide to completing P11D
P4	New employers – starter pack
IR36	Approved profit sharing schemes
IR53	Thinking of taking someone on?
IR56	The employed or self-employed

IR69   Dispensations

Tax tables
A   Free pay tables
B–D   Taxable pay tables
F   Ready Reckoner for codes with prefix 'F'
G   Tax tables for free of tax cases
RDI   Specifications for employer's PAYE substitute end-of-year documents

Leaflets from DHSS

NP 15   Employer's Guide to National Insurance Contributions

NI 227   Employer's Guide to Statutory Sick Pay

NI 257   Employer's Guide To Statutory Sick Pay

NI 35   National Insurance Contributions for Company Directors

CF 391   National Insurance Contributions – Not Contracted Out

CF 392   National Insurance Contributions – Contracted Out

SSP55   SSP Rates and Notes

RD 343   Extra Guidance for Employers who Pay Tax Centrally

RD1(MT)   Specification for Employer's PAYE Substitute End-of-year Documents. Version dealing with returns on magnetic tape

NI1216   Completing your Employees' End-of-year Returns

Forms to use at particular times

Forms you may have to use when new employees start

P8   Deductions guide

P11(87)

P13

P15	If they do not give you a P45
P38(S)	If they are students employed in vacations only
P45	From their previous employer or the Unemployment Benefit Office
P46	If they do not give you a P45
P47	

Forms you may have to use each pay day

P8	Deductions Guide
P11(87)	
Tax Tables	
NI	Contribution tables

Forms you may have to use at the end of the year

P8	Deductions Guide
P9D	
P11(87)	
P11D	
P11D (b)	
P11D	Guide
P13	
P14	
P35	
P35(Z)	
P35(MT)	

P35X

P39

P46(car)

P60

P61

P62

Forms you may have to use when employees leave

P8 Deductions Guide

P11(87)

P13

P45

P160

5
Employee Relations

The role of trade unions

A trade union is defined in law as ' . . . an organisation . . . whose principal purposes include the regulation of relations between workers and employers or between workers and employers' associations . . . ' Some of the larger trade unions, for example the Transport and General Workers Union (TGWU), may have a number of different sections which may be considered to be trade unions in their own right under the law (Trade Union and Labour Relations Act 1974 (TULRA 1974)).

Trade unions may not normally be corporate bodies or be treated as such, but they are given certain features of corporate bodies, namely the power to make contracts and to sue and be sued. Under the provisions of TULRA 1974, the Certification Officer maintains lists of trade unions (see Chapter 8, page 163, for the role of the Certification Officer), entry to which is voluntary and simply means that the particular trade union meets the relevant definitions in law. However, whether listed or not, trade unions are expected to maintain proper accounts and to submit annually to the Certification Officer a return of their affairs, including their audited accounts.

Certificate of independence

In order to acquire legal rights as a trade union once recognised (and to help reinforce any claim to recognition by an employer), a trade union must be independent. TULRA 1974 defines an independent trade union as one which is not under the domination or control of an employer, group of employers or employers' association, and not liable to interference from such quarters (arising out of financial or material support or by any other means whatsoever) tending towards such control. The granting or refusal of a certificate is deemed to be conclusive evidence of the independence or otherwise of the trade union concerned. A trade union refused a certificate may appeal to the Employment Appeal Tribunal (EAT). A recognised, independent trade union may receive financial assistance from the Secretary of State for Employment in order to hold a secret postal ballot on matters such as industrial action, amendments to union rules, union elections and union mergers (Employment Act 1980, Trade Union Act 1980).

Trade union recognition

There is no statutory right of recognition. An employer is free to refuse recognition to an independent trade union, even where it has a significant number of members among the employer's workers. The Advisory, Conciliation and Arbitration Service (ACAS) no longer has a statutory role in issues of trade union recognition (Employment Act 1980). An employer's failure to recognise a trade union after an ACAS recommendation to so do can no longer be translated into an award which forms part of the terms and conditions of employment by the Central Arbitration Committee (CAC). (See Chapter 8, page 157, for an explanation of the role and functions of the CAC.)

Recognition of a trade union by an employer is therefore voluntary, *with one exception*. While trade unions have no general legal right to be recognised by an employer, in a 'Transfer of Undertakings' situation (see note in Chapter 3, page 65), the new employer must recognise any trade union already recognised for whatever purposes by the vendor.

ACAS continues to be used on a voluntary basis by employers and trade unions and will carry out investigations as to the level of support among employees and make recommendations. As the second prime directive of ACAS remains 'to encourage the extension of collective bargaining machinery', it is very likely to recommend recognition of a trade union which has a very small membership (a percentage in the mid-20s is not unusual) within a workforce on the basis that membership will always follow recognition. Other bodies exist, such as the Electoral Reform Society, which will carry out an impartial count of trade union membership among employees and make the results known to both parties.

What to include in a recognition agreement

An agreement of this nature should include:

- *The names of the parties making the agreement.* This must be accurate since many trade unions have separate divisions which are trade unions in their own right (eg while an employer may be willing to have SOGAT represent his shopfloor workers, he might not wish to recognise SOGAT-ATAES in the offices).

- *The categories of employees who will be part of the agreement.* Such an agreement might exclude certain departments or persons, eg an agreement covering salaried administrative staff might exclude the personnel department or the secretaries of senior managers.

- *The purposes for which the trade union is recognised.*

    - discipline and grievance issues;
    - health and safety matters;
    - negotiation of terms and conditions;
    - employee representation on specified company committees;
    - the number of shop stewards/employee representatives the company is prepared to accept, the areas within the company they will cover, and the manner in which they will be elected.

    The employer may also wish to set certain eligibility conditions for appointment to the post of shop steward/employee representative, eg a certain minimum service with the company, a clean disciplinary and conduct record. Some companies look for a specified minimum time spent doing the relevant job or similar work. This practice is not uncommon among employers.

    Where numbers or the complexity of trade union-employer business warrant it, full-time senior employee representatives/convenors may be appointed. The employer is normally expected to pay the appointees at the current rate for their job, adjusted in due course by any increases which would have been received had they remained in their old job.

- *The facilities which will be granted to employee representatives/shop stewards.* Examples are: reasonable time off to carry out their industrial relations duties relating to the employer; visits to the site by full-time trade union officials; office space and use of telephone.

- *The manner in which the agreement is expected to operate.* Appropriate procedures for handling grievances, discipline and other matters for which the employer is prepared to recognise the trade union, need to be created or adjusted to accommodate the presence of a recognised trade union henceforth. Once agreed, procedures must be adhered to by both parties. This is particularly pertinent in disputes, where adherence to the procedure will prevent precipitate industrial action before all other means of resolving the issue have been examined.

- *An agreement that the trade union will sit down with other trade unions* (where more than one trade union is recognised) and negotiate with management jointly on matters of common interest.

- *The extent to which a 'status quo' clause will be accepted by both sides.* If the employer wishes to effect changes to working practices and cannot get the agreement of the recognised trade union(s), the matter may be referred to third parties for resolution. This process can be very time-consuming. The 'status quo' clause will indicate how long the employer will allow the old practices to continue before seeking to effect the changes unilaterally. (Some employers prefer to remain silent on this issue.)

- *Provisions for bringing the agreement to an end.* These usually entail giving both parties the right to terminate the agreement with due notice, which should be specified.

Single union agreements

A single union agreement is, as its name suggests, an arrangement where an employer offers recognition and representation rights to one independent trade union only, which will represent employees of varying disciplines and status – for example, the

Electrical Electronic Telecommunication and Plumbing Union (EETPU), which has sections which can cater for skilled, semi-skilled and unskilled manual workers and salaried staff. These agreements are not uncommon in nationalised industries but are now becoming a feature of 'high tech' companies in the private sector. They are particularly sought by employers in 'greenfields' situations (ie where a new plant is being built), although they have met resistance from other trade unions excluded from the new site, where the employer has a multi-site operation and recognises these other trade unions at the other sites (eg The Coca-Cola Company and its new Sheffield site 1988). The Employment Act (EA) 1988, however, effectively removes all statutory support for 'union membership agreements' (closed shops).

Single union agreements are not problem free. There are a number of difficulties which an employer must resolve before entering into such an agreement:

- if the agreement is also intended to be a union membership agreement (closed shop) this can only be done if the required ballot seeking the approval of the affected employees has been carried out (at least 80 per cent of those entitled to vote must approve). However, sections 10 and 11 of the EA 1988 radically alter the legal standing and effect of union membership agreements:
  - Section 10 makes it unlawful to organise or threaten industrial action to establish or maintain any sort of trade union closed shop practice. It does this by removing legal immunity where the reason, or one of the reasons, for industrial action is either that the employer intends to employ someone who is not a member of a trade union or a particular trade union; or to force an employer to discriminate against someone on the same grounds. Subsequent to the EA 1988, where an employer is threatened with industrial action to enforce or maintain any kind of closed shop practice he can get an injunction ordering the trade union(s) to call off this unlawful action. Failure to obey the injunction can lead to the trade union(s) or individuals declared in contempt of court, leaving them liable to any heavy fines or other penalties the court may decide (where fines have wilfully not been paid, trade union assets have been seized). It is also

possible for the employer to claim damages for losses suffered. Any damages awarded against an individual trade union in such cases are limited, depending on its size.
- Section 11 provides that dismissal of an employee for not being a member of a trade union is unfair in all circumstances. This section also gives employees protection in all circumstances against action short of dismissal (eg threats of dismissal or redundancy, transfers, reduced training or promotion opportunities, etc) to compel them to be union members.

The existence of a union membership agreement (closed shop) does not reduce these rights in any way.

Dismissal of any employee for not belonging to a trade union is unfair, irrespective of whether or not he or she works in an approved closed shop. Referral in such cases is to an industrial tribunal, which will require reinstatement, re-engagement or payment of compensation if it finds the dismissal was unfair or that unfair action short of dismissal has been taken.

It would not be unreasonable to conclude that, pursuant to the Employment Act 1988, a union membership agreement (closed shop) has become a legal anachronism and that closed shops may only persist because all the parties involved accept their existence for the time being. A single objection taken to its conclusion (eg from an employee) will shatter such an agreement.

- if the employer ensures that in a non-union membership agreement situation, employees who are members of other independent trade unions which he does not recognise for any negotiating purposes are treated as even-handedly as his employees who are members of the single recognised trades union, then most of the problems which could arise will be mitigated. The respective full-time officials of the other unions may continue to press for some recognition, but outside the craft unions, where members might decide to carry two union memberships in order to preserve their earning power should they leave their current employer, the ACAS adage is correct and membership does tend to follow recognition. In due time, the situation should settle down.

Rights of an independent trade union

An independent trade union that has obtained recognition by an employer for the purposes of collective bargaining for a particular employee group will also incur rights under the Employment Protection Act 1975, as amended, to:

- disclosure of information consultation on redundancies (see Chapter 7 page 139);
- reasonable paid time off for trade union officials (Employment Protection (Consolidation) Act 1978);
- reasonable time off without pay for its members to take part in its activities;
- the appointment of safety representatives and safety committees, shown in the regulations arising from the Health and Safety at Work Act 1974;
- consultation about changes in occupational pension schemes contained in the regulations pertaining to the Social Security Act 1975 and the requirements of the Social Security Act 1985;
- be informed and consulted in a 'transfer of undertakings' (see note in Chapter 3, page 65);
- hold secret ballots on the employer's premises.

In addition to these rights under the law, recognised independent trade unions usually enjoy other rights conferred upon them by a particular employer. These rights may arise from a formal recognition agreement, which may be adjusted and amended from time to time, or may be privileges which have come about merely by 'custom and practice'. (This underlines the importance of the company being aware of decisions, in connection with relationships with trade unions (where recognised), made by middle as well as senior management. An appropriate, yet reasonably flexible industrial relations policy which offers broad guidelines will act as a tripwire and do much to prevent potential problems.) In most instances, recognised independent trade unions will:

- represent individual members of the trade union in grievance or disciplinary matters;
- provide all or most of the employee representation in works councils, joint consultative committees, joint productivity or

- added value schemes, job evaluation arrangements and other forms of employee involvement;
- be active in such areas as canteen and social committees.

It should be noted that where an employer does not formally recognise an independent trade union, but may have informal dealings with a full-time official of that trade union regarding those employees who are members of the union, he has conferred recognition upon that trade union through 'custom and practice' – at least for the purposes of the arrangement. Where the relationship has proved fruitful, and to the benefit of all parties, this may not matter. But if the trade union wished to extend its activities with the employer at some future date, it would be difficult for him in logic to reject these overtures. He could do so legally, however, although at some cost to good employee relations.

Rights of individual employees and trade union membership

It is as well to remind ourselves at this stage what the rights of individual employees are in relation to trade union membership. Individuals may be said to have two distinct rights relating to this issue:

- the right to belong to and take part in the activities of an independent trade union;
- the right not to belong to a trade union.

In each case, however, it is an indirect right and is limited in extent as the ultimate remedy for infringement of these rights, should the employer prove to be intransigent (in certain instances a trade union may be co-joined), in monetary compensation. In cases of (unfair) action short of dismissal, awards can range from £50 for 'frustration and stress' to whatever the industrial tribunal deems appropriate in the circumstances (ie no upper limit). Where unfair dismissal is established on these grounds, compensation in extreme cases (long service employee, pension loss, employer refusing an order to reinstate or re-engage, etc) can approach £40,000.

Possible stages of trade union recognition

Many employers, when asked to recognise an independent trade union for the first time, may be hesitant to enter into a full agreement until they have had time to gauge exactly what is involved in practice. (They must be absolutely clear whom among their employees the trade union is seeking to represent.)

As an alternative, and informing the trade union of the reasons for the strategy, full recognition may be approached in the following manner:

(a) granting certain rights to the trade union such as the use of part of the notice board, entry to site to address employees at appropriate times (eg meal breaks);
(b) permitting the trade union to represent members in discipline and grievance cases;
(c) negotiating with the trade union on pay and conditions.

However, it would be very difficult to reverse this process once it is embarked upon and employers should be aware of this. It would not be unreasonable for an employer to require proof that the trade union had a significant majority of members among the relevant employee group for which it was seeking recognition. If this should be the case, then a more graduated approach to full recognition would have to start at step (b), if adopted at all.

Employee involvement initiatives

These can either come about either from trade union demand and company concession, or be part of a proactive personnel/industrial relations policy arising from the company's decision to recognise the trade union. In the latter case, it is probable that the employer already operates, either formally or informally, consultative machinery and channels of information with his employees. In the new climate brought about by recognition of an independent trade union, these arrangements will need formalising and appropriate terms of reference and rules of conduct drawn up.

A 'works committee' (or council)

This is a good basis for an exchange of relevant information and opinions. Its membership should not be confined to trade union members, but should include a cross section of the total workforce. Minutes of the works committee meetings should be taken and published to employees. While it is common that the chairmanship of this meeting is retained by the company, this is not the only practice to be found (eg some works committees have joint chairmen and rotate the chair; others have a senior employee representative/convenor as deputy chairman who will chair the meeting in the absence of the chairman, etc). It is also quite usual that the task of secretary to the works committe/council is carried out on a joint basis by the convenor or a senior employee representative and a member of management in order to ensure agreement of the minutes. From this committee/council can flow various sub-committees which can deal with joint productivity or added value schemes, employee job evaluation, and special purpose or special project work where a joint consultative approach would prove worthwhile.

Safety committee

With the agreement of the recognised independent trade union(s), it may be possible to retain a full cross section of the workforce, union and non-union employees, on the company safety committee. Under the Health and Safety at Work Act 1974 and the 1977 Regulations pertaining to safety representatives and safety committees, only members of recognised trade unions have the right to be safety representatives. If two or more safety representatives request to set up a safety committee, in writing, the employer must comply within three months. The size of that committee should be decided by joint consultation to ensure its efficient operation. If the recognised trade union(s) so wished, it could reserve all seats on the committee (bar those held by management) to itself and exclude all non-union employees. In such a circumstance, the employer would have to establish parallel avenues of communication and consultation with non-union employees. Many companies have managed to retain safety committees whose membership reflects the total workforce.

Briefing groups

These are another channel of communication with employees. They operate on a cascade basis from the most senior executive on site, down through management and supervision to the shop floor. The information which the company wishes to impart is usually prepared as a written brief with answers provided for likely questions which might arise. At each level the briefing is given, questions answered and comment received. In this way, a message is made common knowledge quickly and management receives immediate reaction from the widest possible audience. Many companies do this informally with varying success. To gain any lasting benefit the briefing system must be done well, which means that briefing managers and supervisors must be given training. They must be able to make a presentation and, for example, have the wit to note and refer questions they cannot answer rather than guess.

Meetings with recognised trade union representatives/shop stewards

In addition to the various committees which they might attend, these representatives will wish to raise particular union business concerning their membership either individually or collectively with management. It may be possible that where more than one trade union is recognised and matters of common interest are concerned, the employer may deal with the trade unions jointly. This is an important condition for a recognition agreement, even where only one trade union is to be recognised at that time.

Employee involvement

Employee involvement can be a progression in itself. It happens informally to a greater or lesser degree in all work situations. It is usually covered in these circumstances by the blanket term 'communications', where information tends to flow down from the employer to the shopfloor and the former tries to identify 'opinion-makers' among the workforce to use as sounding boards. The success of the majority of such systems can be judged by the given response to a general question, 'How are communications in this company?' Where printable, it is usually believed by the workforce that key information is being withheld and/or their views ignored in varying degrees by the employer. Communications can be formalised and improved by using efficient briefing groups and the various committees on site, but care should be taken not to degrade their function by dealing with trivia.

The next stage is *consultation*, where an issue is raised by the employer and thrown open to general discussion with employees. Having presented the relevant facts and listened to the range of views offered, the employer makes the decision. Employees are kept abreast of progress as matters develop. This process can be further refined into project work, where people with expertise gained from relevant experience, training and formal qualifications come together as a vertical slice of the organisation to examine a particular development, need or problem and make recommendations to the employer, who makes the final decision.

Finally, there is *participation*, where the full process basic and/or refined of consultation is carried out but, ultimately, a decision is made jointly by employer and employees. This not a common practice in the United Kingdom, except in certain companies run on a communal basis. A number of other companies have 'worker directors' as part of their management boards, who are trade union nominees elected by the membership within the company to the post. These have not led to radical changes in the way their companies have been managed. The worker directors were looked upon in their time as the forerunners of a new form of 'industrial democracy'. Little has been heard on this topic since the Bullock Report of the mid-1970s, but arrangements of this nature are more common in EC countries and enabling legislation continues to progress slowly, with much modification and amendment, through the European Parliament.

Trade disputes

In the event that a dispute arises between the employer and a recognised trade union, and it appears to the trade union that the issue is unlikely to be resolved when the disputes procedure is exhausted, it may wish to be able to initiate industrial action including strike action at that point. The Trade Union Act 1984 (Part II) requires the trade union to hold a secret ballot in which all those required to take part in the action are entitled to vote. Where the recognised trade union wishes to hold such a secret ballot on site and makes the necessary request to the employer, it should be complied with unless it is not 'reasonably practicable'. The ballot should take place not more than four weeks before the start of the industrial action.

In British employment law there is no *right to strike*. However, the law provides immunity from civil liability for certain torts or actions likely to occur during the progress of a dispute. But this dispensation only applies where:

- the strike action has been endorsed by a majority of affected union members in a pre-strike ballot;
- the action is taken directly against the employer with whom the members in dispute have their contracts of employment.

Protection is not extended to secondary action which is designed to put direct pressure on the employer who is party to the dispute.

Picketing

The Trade Unions and Labour Relations Act (TULRA) 1974 and the Employment Act 1980 define the rules for lawful industrial picketing, which may only be:

- undertaken in contemplation or furtherance of a trade dispute;
- performed by a person attending at or near his own place of work (or former place of work), or a person without a fixed place of work who pickets the place from which his work is administered, or a trade union official accompanying a member;
- done in order peacefully to obtain or communicate information, or peacefully persuade a person to work or not to work.

Note. Statutory protection is only conferred by the Employment Act 1980 to 'peaceful picketing in contemplation of furtherance of a trade dispute'.

The Department of Employment has produced a Code of Practice on picketing which came into effect on 17 December 1980. It offers practical guidance to those considering taking such action in furtherance of a trade dispute and to those employers, workers or other third parties who might be affected by the picketing. It suggests that in general the number of pickets used does not exceed six at any one entrance to a workplace, and that frequently a smaller number would suffice since the purpose of the picketing is peaceful persuasion and not mass intimidation.

If the picketing does not conform to the law, an employer or employee (whose contract has been interfered with by such action) has a civil law remedy. He or she may seek an injunction through the courts to stop the unlawful picketing and can start an action for damages.

Strikes and the contract of employment

A work stoppage (strike) is a breach of contract by the individual employee. It is held in law to be so fundamental that it allows the employer to dismiss summarily without giving notice. An employee so dismissed is not able to claim unfair dismissal, provided the employer observes certain conditions in re-employing those who went on strike. These conditions are that:

- there was an industrial action which led to a breach of contract;
- the dismissal took place while the action was taking place, not before or after;
- all relevant employees (ie those taking part in the action at the complainant's date of dismissal) were dismissed. Those employees who may have participated in the industrial action but heeded a warning from the employer to return to work or be dismissed fall outside the 'relevant employees' definition and cannot be cited by the complainant;
- no relevant employees are re-engaged within a period of three months after the date of dismissal.

The time limit for making a claim for unfair dismissal in a strike or other industrial action is six months from the date of dismissal (excluding notice) and recourse is to an industrial tribunal.

Resolution of industrial disputes

The Advisory, Conciliation and Arbitration Service is charged by the Employment Protection Act 1975 to offer and provide assistance in the solution of an industrial dispute by conciliation or by other means. ACAS will seek to encourage both parties to a dispute to make proper use of any agreed procedures appropriate to the situation and its resolution. If the issue cannot be resolved using conciliation, then at the request of either party but with the consent of both, ACAS may refer the matter to an independent arbiter or arbiters or to the Central Arbitration Committee (see also Chapter 8, page 157). There is no legal obligation on the parties to accept an arbitrator's decision, but acceptance is usually the case.

The CAC will also provide unilateral arbitration in relation to the provisions on disclosure of information to trade unions for collective bargaining purposes. Similar provisions exist for unilateral arbitration under the Equal Pay Act 1970.

The traditional task of an arbitrator has been to effect a compromise between what the employer was prepared to offer and what the trade union sought ('pendulum arbitration'). A new feature of recent industrial relations practice has been the acceptance by both parties of pendulum arbitration as a final stage in a dispute. Under this process the independent arbitrator decides for the employer or the trade union without compromise.

Payment during a strike

There is no obligation on the employer to pay employees when they are on strike.

Continuous employment

Participating in a strike will not normally break an employee's period of continuous service with the employer as far as statutory rights are concerned. However, the weeks during which the employee was on strike or locked out do not count in calculating length of service for statutory benefits, eg redundancy payments where such time deductions might be crucial in deciding if benefit will be paid and, if, so how much.

6
Health and Safety at Work

The Health and Safety at Work Act (HASAWA) 1974

Main purposes
The main purposes of the Act are as follows:

- to promote and secure the health, safety and welfare of people at work (including Youth Training Scheme and Job Training Scheme trainees while at the workplace);
- to protect others from risks arising from the activities of people at work;
- to control the storage and use of dangerous substances and to prevent the unlawful acquisition, possession and use of such substances;
- to prevent the emission into the atmosphere of noxious or offensive substances.

The 1974 Act is an enabling measure superimposed on existing health and safety legislation – for example the Factories Act 1971, Offices Shops & Railway Premises Act 1963, etc remain in force and their provisions continue for the time being. There are 31 relevant Acts and some 500 subsidiary regulations involved. The aim of HASAWA 1974 is to promote greater awareness of safety among the population at large and to promote high standards of health and safety at work. It seeks to do this by creating one comprehensive and integrated system of law to deal with this need. Regulations, codes of practice and guidance notes arising from the 1974 Act provide a framework from which means to improve standards and practices emerge. The legislation is administered by the Health and Safety Commission and the Safety Executive.

HASAWA 1974 covers all 'persons at work', whether

employers, self-employed or employees (including trainees while at the workplace) with the exception of domestic servants in a private household.

Health and safety requirements for the protection of workers are either *absolute* (eg 'an employer shall . . . '), thereby imposing a statutory duty on employers in the circumstances at which the regulations are directed, or *qualified* by such wording as 'as far as is reasonably practicable'. The 1974 Act is enforced by the Health and Safety Inspectors of the Health & Safety Executive.

General duties of the employer

HASAWA 1974 starts from the premise that there are general duties on employers in regard to their employees which are laid down under previous legislation dealing with the health, safety and welfare of people at work. Much of the earlier law is retained, but the method of enforcement has changed and the powers of inspectors increased. Where the 1974 Act has imposed new responsibilities, they apply universally.

These general duties are defined in broad terms as 'an employer must safeguard, so far as is reasonably practicable, the health, safety and welfare of all his employees while they are at work'. In particular, he must provide:

- a safe place to work;
- safe means of access to the workplace;
- safe systems of work and associated plant;
- safe usage, handling, storage and transport of materials and substances;
- adequate information, instruction, training and supervision.

In addition, the employer must:

- publish a written statement of his general policy, organisation and arrangements for health and safety at work, and maintain its currency (this applies to employers with five or more employees);
- set up a safety committee if trade union appointed safety representatives request it (only an independent, recognised trade union may exercise this right).

Duties of employees

While at work, employees have a duty under the 1974 Act to:

- take reasonable care to avoid injury to themselves or to others by their work activities;
- co-operate with their employer and/or any other person in meeting the statutory requirements.

Employees must not interfere with or misuse anything provided to protect their health, safety or welfare in compliance with the Act.

Section 9 of the Act prohibits an employer levying any charge on an employee in respect of anything done or provided to satisfy any specific requirements of health, safety and welfare legislation.

Duties to persons other than employees

Under the Act, the employer has duties for the protection of persons other than his employees (eg members of the public) to:

- conduct his business in such a manner as to ensure that, so far as is reasonably practicable, persons not in his employment are not exposed to risks to their health or safety;
- give information in prescribed circumstances to persons who are not his employees about such aspects of the manner in which he conducts his business as might affect their health or safety.

(Regulations will be made prescribing the circumstances and the information required.)

General duties in relation to premises

The 1974 Act imposes duties on persons in relation to those who (a) are not their employees; but (b) use non-domestic premises made available to them as a place of work, or as a place where they may use plant or substances provided for their use there. Where a person has, due to any contract or tenancy, any obligation in relation to:

- maintenance or repair of the premises and the means of access thereto, or
- the safety of or the absence of risks to health arising from plant or substances in such premises,

he shall be treated as the person responsible for the purposes of the 1974 Act.

This is a general provision and the person in control of premises may also have other duties under other enactments, eg fire precautions, public health etc.

Section 5 of the Act deals with emission of noxious or offensive substances into the atmosphere and places duties of prevention or rendering such substances harmless on those in control of premises.

Duties of manufacturers and suppliers of articles and substances for use at work

The Act places duties on persons who:

- design, manufacture, import, supply, erect or install any article, plant, machinery, equipment or appliances for use at work, or
- manufacture, import or supply any substance for use at work.

It also places duties for research on designers and manufacturers.

Every employer is likely to be affected by these provisions as a purchaser and user of articles and substances, and many will also bear duties as described below.

An 'article for use at work' is defined as (a) any plant, machinery, equipment or appliance designed for use or operation (whether exclusively or not) by persons at work, and (b) any article designed for use as a component in any such plant.

A 'substance for use at work' is any natural or artificial substance whether in solid or liquid form, or in the form of a gas or vapour intended for use (whether exclusively or not) by persons at work.

General duties (articles)
It shall be the duty of any person who designs, manufactures, imports or supplies any article for use at work to:

- ensure, so far as is reasonably practicable, that the article is of safe design and construction and carries no risk to health when properly used;
- carry out or arrange for the carrying out of such tests as may be required by the preceding paragraph;
- provide adequate instructions and information about the safe usage of the article at work.

Requirements for research
Section 6 states that any person who designs or manufactures any article for use at work must carry out, or make arrangements for carrying out, any necessary research seeking to eliminate or minimise any risk to health or safety to which the design or article may give rise.

Erection and installation
Any person who erects or installs any article for use at work in any premises where that article is to be used by persons, has a duty to ensure, so far as is reasonably practicable, that nothing about the way it has been erected or installed makes it unsafe or a risk to health when properly used.

General duties (substances)
It is the duty of any person who manufactures, imports or supplies any substance for use at work to:

- ensure, so far as is reasonably practicable, that the substance is safe and without risk to health when properly used;
- carry out, or arrange to be carried out, such tests as may be necessary to satisfy the requirements of the preceding paragraph;
- provide adequate information and instructions about the safe usage of the substance at work.

Requirement for research
Manufacturers are responsible for undertaking any such research as necessary to eliminate or minimise any risks to health and safety to which a substance may give rise. However, they are not required to repeat any tests or research carried out by a reputable third party whose results may be relied upon for the purposes of the Act's provisions.

Company reports

The Companies Act 1967 is amended by the 1974 Act (Section 79) to require companies, in classes to be prescribed by regulations, to include in their directors' reports information on health and safety. These must include details about the arrangements effective in that year for securing the health, safety and welfare at work of company employees and those of any subsidiary companies, and for protecting other persons against risks to health or safety arising out of or in connection with the activities of those employees.

Enforcement of HASAWA 1974 associated legislation

Powers of inspectors
The powers of an inspector enable him to carry out his duties under the Act (Section 20). They include:

- power to enter, at any reasonable time, any premises which he has reason to believe it is necessary for him to enter for the purpose of carrying into effect any of the legal provisions within his remit;
- taking with him any duly authorised person and any equipment that he requires. He may take measurements, photographs and recordings that are necessary for any examination or investigation;
- taking samples, having the authority to require any person to give him information relevant to his examination or investigation, to answer questions and to sign a declaration of the truth of his answers;
- requiring any person to afford him such facilities and assistance, within that person's control or responsibilities, as are necessary to enable the inspector to exercise any of the powers conferred on him.
- bringing prosecutions for unsafe practices.

The additional powers conferred on inspectors by the 1974 Act permit them to:

- issue prohibition notices, which have the immediate effect of stopping machinery or a process until the remedial action specified in the notice has been taken;
- issue improvement notices, which require an employer to remedy specific problems within a specific time;
- prosecute any person contravening a relevant statutory provision, instead of or in addition to serving a notice.

Inspectors may also 'after prior consultation with the persons on the spot' seize, render harmless, or destroy any article or substance that might be the cause of imminent danger or serious personal injury.

An inspector is appointed in writing by his enforcing authority and must when required to do so produce a copy of his instrument of appointment.

Disclosure of information
The Act (Section 28(8)) imposes duties upon inspectors to disclose certain information to employees (or their trade union representatives where applicable) at premises to which the Act applies to assist in keeping them adequately informed of matters likely to affect their health, safety and welfare. This duty is in addition to that placed on the employer, and may include factual information obtained by the inspector which relates to the premises or anything being done there. In addition, the inspector may give information concerning any action he has taken, or proposes to take, in or in connection with the premises. The inspector is required to give the employer the same information as he gives to employees.

Breaches of the Act
Breaches of HASAWA 1974 can result in prosecution in magistrates courts (or their equivalent in Scotland). As criminal law, penalties for breaches can be imposed by the Courts. Claims against employers for compensation for injury or industrial disease arising out of the failure to observe a statutory requirement (but not a HASAWA 1974 requirement), or failing to observe the Common Law (for example the duty of care), have to be pursued separately in civil actions. The result can therefore be separate actions against an employer arising out of the same alleged breach, with the record of a criminal conviction being admissible in the civil proceedings.

The Health and Safety Commission (HSC)
The commission consists of representatives of both sides of industry and the local authorities. It has taken over from government departments the responsibility for developing policies in the health and safety field (see also Chapter 8, page 158).

The Health and Safety Executive (HSE)
This is a separate statutory body appointed by the Commission which will work in accordance with directions and guidance given by the Commission. The Executive will also enforce legal requirements, as well as provide an advisory service to both

employers and trade unions. The major inspectorates in the health and safety field have been brought within the Executive instead of being scattered and working independently within several government departments.

Employment Medical Advisory Service (EMAS)

This service will act as the medical arm of the Commission. It will be the main channel of medical advice to the Commission and to the Inspectorate within the Executive. The scope of the service is not substantially altered by the 1974 Act, but it has become more directly involved in giving advice over the whole range of the Commission's activities. It is also involved in work for which there has been no previous statutory responsibility but which comes within the scope of the Commission and the Inspectorates, laboratories and research establishments, for example. It continues to give medical advice to the various divisions of the Training Commission. Employment Medical Advisers continue to provide clinical medical attention in skills centres and industrial rehabilitation units. ACAS uses EMAS as a source of advice about medical matters relating to industrial relations.

Safety representatives

Provided they are members of recognised, independent trade unions, safety representatives are able to:

- represent employees in consultations with the employer;
- make representations on matters of health and safety at work which affect (a) their members, and (b) persons employed at their place of work;
- carry out inspections;
- represent their members in consultations with officers of the Health and Safety Executive;
- receive information from inspectors;
- attend safety committee meetings;
- investigate potential hazards and dangerous occurrences at the workplace.

Every three months *workplace inspections* should be permitted, provided written notice has been given or where:

- there has been a substantial change in the conditions of work, or

- any notifiable accident occurs.

Documents which the employer is required by law to keep may also be inspected. Employers must provide facilities and assistance as 'reasonably required' by safety representatives for the purpose of carrying out their functions.

Safety policies

A safety policy should be a statement of intent by the employer to provide safe and healthy working conditions. The duty to prepare and update as necessary such a policy rests on all employers, bar those who employ less than five employees. The exemption exists because where there are few employees it is assumed that communication is by word of mouth rather than in writing The policy should name the person ultimately responsible for the policy (preferably a board member), the names of others with specific responsibilities (eg safety officers), and a statement of their duties. It should also ensure that those who work at risk understand the hazards, and that individual employees understand their part in maintaining a safe and healthy place of work.

As breaches of safety rules are also breaches of contracts of employment, it is essential that individual employees are aware of safety policy statements and any revisions to them. It is recommended that the statements form part of the induction process and that relevant updates are issued to individuals where practicable. Inclusion in employee handbooks and/or broadsheets setting out works rules, or as an annexe to individual contracts of employment, will also help. The aim is to ensure that more is done than putting up a notice, however prominently.

First-aid

The Health and Safety (First-Aid) Regulations came into operation in 1981. The Health and Safety Commission has published an approved code of practice to accompany these regulations. All employers, employees and self-employed persons are covered by the regulations, except in the case of certain diving operations, vessels, mines and military forces (Regulation 7).

Duty of the employer
The employer must provide, or ensure that there are provided,

such equipment and facilities as are adequate and appropriate in the circumstances for enabling first-aid to be rendered to his employees if they are injured or become ill at work, for example:

(a) Provision of a suitable number of trained first-aiders who must have:
- HSE approved qualifications and training;
- such additional training as may be appropriate.

(b) The appointment of a person* (which is sufficient compliance for the requirement when a first-aider is absent) to:
- take charge of a situation involving an injured or sick employee who will need help from a medical practitioner or nurse;
- take charge of the equipment and facilities provided by the company throughout the period of absence.

(c) Where the nature of the premises and the number of employees mean that a person suitable to render first-aid under (b) above would be sufficient, then such a person may be appointed instead of a first-aider.

(d) Provision of facilities and equipment: when deciding what equipment and facilities are needed, the employer should have regard for:
- the number of employees;
- the nature of the undertaking;
- the size of the establishment and the distribution of employees;
- the location of the establishment and the locations to which employees go in the course of their work.

Number of employees
When determining the total numbers of first-aiders needed, the employer should take account of the following factors:

* An 'appointed person' is someone provided by the employer to take charge of the situation when serious injury or major illness occurs in the absence of a first-aider or occupational first-aider (eg to call an ambulance). An appointed person is also responsible for first-aid equipment in the absence of a first-aider or occupational first-aider.

- the number of employees at work;
- the nature of the work undertaken;
- the extent to which employees are working in scattered locations;
- working patterns, namely day work, double day shift, three shifts, mixture etc;
- distance from outside medical services.

As a guide, it is recommended that in an area of low hazard (for instance office, shop, bank, library) the ratio of first-aiders to employees should be 1:150.

For any establishment with a greater degree of hazard (eg factory, dockyard, warehouse, farm), the employer should ensure that there is at least one first-aider present when the number of employees at work is between 50 and 150. Where there are more than 150 employees at work, there should be at least one other first-aider for every additional 150 employees.

Where there are fewer than 150 employees in a low hazard establishment, or less than 50 employees in any other place of work, there may be no need for a first-aider. If the employer does not provide one, however, he must provide an appointed person at all times when employees are at work.

In establishments presenting special or unusual hazards, employers should provide more than the recommended minimum of first-aiders, and provide at least one occupational first-aider (see page 118 for definition of first-aiders).

Where there is shift working, employers should ensure that sufficient first-aiders are appointed to provide adequate cover for each shift in relation to the number of employees at work on the shift.

First-aid room

Where 400 or more employees are at work in an establishment, the employer should provide a properly equipped and staffed first-aid room. In cases where there are special hazards, a first-aid room would be appropriate for establishments with considerably fewer employees.

Where a first-aid room is appropriate for an establishment the following conditions should be met:

- A suitably qualified person should be responsible for the room and its contents.

- A first-aider/occupational first-aider should be nearby or on call at all times when employees are at work.
- A room should be readily available at all times when employees are at work. It should be used for the sole purpose of rendering first-aid.
- It should be positioned as near as possible to a point of access for transport to a hospital.
- It should contain suitable facilities and equipment. The room should be well lit, heated, ventilated and maintained. All surfaces should be easy to clean.
- It should be sufficiently large to contain a couch with space for people to work around it.
- The door should be large enough to allow access for a stretcher, wheelchair, carrying chair or wheeled carriage.
- Suitable waiting facilities (eg chairs) should be provided close to the first-aid room.
- The room should be clearly identified and designated as a first-aid room.
- There should be a note attached to the door of the first-aid room showing the names and locations of the first-aiders, occupational first-aiders and appointed persons, and the times when they are available.
- Effective means of communication should exist between all work areas and the first-aid room, and the first-aider/occupational first-aider on call.

Employees who work away from the normal establishment
An employer may not need to make additional provisions for employees working away from his establishment, other than permanent provision for his workforce at that establishment to include itinerant employees working in urban areas whose work involves sales, delivery, inspection or other similar work with relatively low hazards.

Employees should be provided with small travelling first aid kits, if they work alone or in small groups and:

(a) work in isolated locations (eg forestry, agriculture, railway and other maintenance jobs);
(b) travel long distances in remote areas in which access to National Health Service accident and emergency facilities may be difficult; or

(c) use potentially dangerous tools or machinery.

If their work involves the use of potentially hazardous tools and machinery, and taking into account the numbers involved and the hazards and location it may be necessary to provide, or ensure that there is provided at the respective work locations, other first-aid equipment – even first-aid facilities and personnel.

First-aid boxes and kits

First-aid boxes and small travelling kits should contain an adequate quantity of suitable first-aid materials and nothing else.

The contents of these boxes or kits should be replenished as soon as possible after use to ensure that there is always an adequate supply of materials available. Also, since some materials deteriorate with age, these will need to be replaced from time to time. It is essential that first-aid boxes and kits are checked regularly.

The contents of first-aid boxes and travelling kits are laid down by the Regulations. The box should be made of suitable material which will protect the contents from damp and dust. It should be clearly marked so that it can be identified readily, the recommended marking being a white cross on a green background. The box should contain only the prescribed items shown on page 119 (the number of items is dependent on the number of people employed).

Suitable persons for first-aiders

First-aiders
These are people who:

- have been trained and hold a current first-aid certificate issued by an organisation or employer whose training and qualifications for first-aiders were, at the time of issue of the certificate, approved by the HSE for the purposes of the Regulations;
- hold a current first-aid certificate issued up to three years before the operation of the First-Aid Regulations 1981 by an organisation or employer whose training and qualifications for occupational first-aiders given during that period have been approved by the HSE for the purposes of these Regulations.

Item	Number of employees				
	1–5	*6–10*	*11–20*	*51–100*	*101–150*
First-aid guidance card	1	1	1	1	1
Individually wrapped sterile adhesive dressings	10	20	40	40	40
Sterile eye pads with attachment	1	2	4	6	8
Triangular bandages	1	2	4	6	8
Safety pins	6	6	12	12	12
Sterile unmedicated dressings:					
– medium	3	6	8	10	12
– large	1	2	4	6	10
– extra large	1	2	4	6	8

First aid boxes and kits

Occupational first-aiders
These are first-aiders who:

- have been trained and hold a current occupational first-aid certificate issued by an organisation or employer whose training and qualifications for occupational first-aiders were, at the time of issue of the certificate, approved by the HSE for the purposes of the Regulations;
- hold a current occupational first-aid certificate issued up to three years before the operation of the First-Aid Regulations 1981 by an organisation or employer whose training and qualifications for occupational first-aiders given during that period has been approved by the HSE for the purposes of the

Regulations, and who may have received specialised instruction concerning the particular first-aid requirements of the employer's undertaking.

Other persons
These people have undergone training and obtained qualifications approved by the HSE for the purposes of the Regulations. Such people may act as first-aiders or occupational first-aiders.

Duty of employers to inform employees of first-aid arrangements

Regulation 4 states that 'an employer shall inform his employees of the arrangements that have been made in connection with the provision of first-aid, including the location of equipment, facilities and personnel.' The HSE code of practice recommends that employers should:

- tell new employees of the location of the first-aid equipment and personnel;
- ensure that they are familiar with the location of facilities when they first join the establishment;
- post at least one notice in a prominent position at all workplaces within the establishment (including any central office from which itinerant employees go out to work), giving the locations of first-aid equipment and facilities and the names and locations of personnel concerned;
- ensure that the notices are in English and that a translation is provided in any other language commonly used at the establishment; this may be displayed alongside the English version.

Notices which must be displayed by the employer

Under HASAWA 1974, every employer who employs five or more people must prepare and publish a written statement of his general policy on health and safety.

As we have seen, the Health and Safety (First-Aid) Regulations 1981 demand that employers must post notices in English and any other language in common use at the workplace. In addition to this requirement, employers must display the following notices:

- A copy of the certificate of insurance (Employer's Liability (Compulsory Insurance) Act 1969).
- In factories:
  - Form F1 (prescribed abstract in the Factories Act 1961);
  - the address of the HSE inspector for the district and the superintending inspector of the division;
  - the name and address of the employment medical adviser for the area;
  - Form F11 specifying the hours of employment of young persons for each day of the week and including details of the meal and rest intervals;
  - printed copies of any relevant regulations in force at the time or prescribed abstracts of those regulations (information about the special regulations relating to particular processes and applying to particular industries is available from the HSE);
- In office, shops and on railway premises:
  - A copy of the Offices, Shops and Railway Premises Act 1963 and a thermometer, which can be read easily, sited on each floor.
- In shops:
  - Details about the hours of young persons and a notice specifying the days of the week in which shop assistants are not employed after 13.30 hours.

Notification of injuries, diseases and dangerous occurrences

Under the Reporting of Injuries, Diseases and Dangerous Occurrences Regulations 1985 (effective from 1 April 1986), employers and self-employed persons must notify the enforcing authority by *the quickest practicable means* if any person, as a result of an accident arising out of or in connection with work, dies or suffers any of the injuries or conditions (See 'Reportable injuries and conditions' below), or where there is a dangerous occurrence (see 'Dangerous occurrences', page 123). (The 'quickest practicable means' might be by telephone, the caller giving his name and noting the name of the person who answers the call.) Within seven days of a dangerous occurrence happening, the responsible person must send a report of it to the enforcing authority on a form available from the HSE.

Reportable injuries and conditions
These are:

(a) Fractures of the skull, spine or pelvis.
(b) Fracture of any bone:
   – in the arm or wrist, but not a bone in the hand, or
   – in the leg or ankle, but not a bone in the foot.
(c) Amputation of:
   – a hand or foot, or
   – a finger, thumb or toe, or any part thereof if the joint or bone is completely severed.
(d) The loss of sight of an eye, a penetrating injury to an eye, or a chemical or hot metal burn to an eye.
(e) Injury (including burns) requiring immediate medical treatment, or loss of consciousness, resulting in either case from an electric shock from any electrical circuit or equipment whether or not due to direct contact.
(f) Loss of consciousness resulting from lack of oxygen.
(g) Decompression sickness (unless suffered during an operation to which the Diving Operations at Work Regulations 1981 apply) requiring immediate medical treatment.
(h) Acute illness requiring medical treatment, or loss of consciousness, resulting in either case from the absorption of any substance by inhalation, ingestion or through the skin.
(i) Acute illness requiring medical treatment where there is reason to believe that this resulted from exposure to a pathogen or infected material.
(j) Any other injury which results in the injured person being admitted immediately to hospital for more than 24 hours.

Reporting

In addition, if a person at work is incapacitated for work of a kind which he might reasonably be expected to do, either under his contract of employment or, if there is no such contract, in the normal course of his work, for more than three consecutive days (excluding the day of the accident but including any days which would not have been working days) because of an injury, other than one specified above (see 'Reportable injuries and conditions'), resulting from an accident at work, the responsible person shall within seven days of the accident send a report thereof to the enforcing authority on an approved HSE form.

A further requirement is that if an employee, as a result of an accident at work, has suffered a reportable injury or condition which is a cause of his death within one year of the date of that accident, the employer must inform the enforcing authority in writing of the death as soon as it comes to his knowledge.

An immediate report is required if a person suffers from one of 42 diseases or conditions listed in Schedule 2 to the Regulations and his work involves one of the activities specified therein (eg occupational deafness; pneumoconiosis (coal mines or quarries) etc).

Dangerous occurrences
These are as follows:

(a) *Breathing apparatus.* Any incident where breathing apparatus, being worn to enable the user to breathe independently of the surrounding environment, malfunctions in a manner which will deprive the user of oxygen or expose him to a contaminated atmosphere, so posing a danger to his health. This paragraph does not apply to such apparatus while it is being:
- used in a mine, or
- maintained or tested.

(b) *Collapse of building or structure.* Any unintended collapse or partial collapse of:
- any building or structure under construction, reconstruction, alteration or demolition, or of any false work, involving a fall of more than five tonnes of material, or
- any floor or wall of any building being used as a place of work, not being a building under construction, reconstruction, alteration or demolition.

(c) *Collapse of scaffolding.* A collapse or partial collapse of any scaffold which is more than 5m high which results in a substantial part of the scaffold falling or overturning. Also, where the scaffold is slung or suspended, a collapse or part collapse of the suspension arrangements (including any outrigger) which causes a working platform or cradle to fall more than 5m.

(d) *Conveyance of dangerous substances by road.* Any incident in which a road tanker or tank container (as defined in the

Dangerous Substances Conveyance by Road in Road Tankers and Tank Containers Regulations 1981) used for conveying a dangerous substance by road:
- overturns, or
- suffers serious damage to the tank in which the dangerous substance is being conveyed, or
- where there is, in relation to such a road tanker or tank container
  - an uncontrolled release or escape of the dangerous substance being conveyed, or
  - a fire which involves a dangerous substance being conveyed.

(e) *Electrical short circuit.* Electrical short circuit or overload attended by fire or explosion which results in the stoppage of the plant involved for more than 24 hours and which, taking into account the circumstances of the occurrence, might have been liable to cause the death of, or any of the injuries or conditions listed under 'Reportable injuries and conditions', page 121 above to any person.

(f) *Escape of flammable substances.* The sudden, uncontrolled release of one tonne or more of flammable liquid, within the meaning of the Highly Flammable Liquids and Liquified Petroleum Gases Regulations 1972, flammable gas or flammable liquid above its boiling point from any plant, system or pipeline.

(g) *Escape of a substance or pathogen.* The uncontrolled or accidental release or the escape of any substance or pathogen from any apparatus, equipment, pipework, pipeline, process plant, storage vessel, tank, in-works conveyance tanker, land-fill site, or exploratory land drilling site which, having regard to the nature of the substance or the pathogen and the extent and the location of the release or escape, might have been liable to cause the death of, or any of the injuries or conditions which are notifiable (see page 121) or other damage to the health of, any person.

(h) *Explosion or fire.* An explosion or fire occurring in any plant or place which results in the stoppage of that plant or suspension from normal work in that place for more than 24 hours, where such explosion or fire was due to the ignition of process materials, their by-products (including waste) or finished products.

(i) *Explosives.* Any ignition or explosion of explosives, where the ignition or explosion was not intentional.

(j) *Freight containers.* Failure of any freight container or failure of any load-bearing part thereof, while it is being raised, lowered or suspended (Freight Containers (Safety Convention) Regulations 1984).

(k) *Gas incidents.* The Gas Safety (Installation and Use) Regulations 1984 lay obligations on two new classes of people:
- those who supply flammable gas to a fixed pipe distribution system, and
- those who fill, import or supply refillable containers of liquified petroleum gas (excluding the retail trade).

(l) *Lifting machinery, etc.* The collapse of, the overturning of, or the failure of any load-bearing part of any:
- lift, hoist, crane, derrick or mobile powered access platform, but not any winch, teagle, pulley block, gin wheel transporter or runway;
- excavator;
- pile-driving frame or rig having an overall height, when operating, of more than 7m.

(m) *Locomotives.* Any case of an accidental collision between a locomotive or a train and any other vehicle at a factory or at dock premises which may have been liable to cause the death of, or any of the notifiable injuries or conditions listed on page 121.

(n) *Overhead electric lines.* Any incident in which plant or equipment either comes into contact with an uninsulated overhead electric line in which the voltage exceeds 200 volts, or causes an electrical discharge from such an electric line by coming into close proximity to it, unless in either case the incident was intentional.

(o) *Passenger-carrying amusement device*. The following incidents at a fun fair (whether or not a travelling fun fair) where the relevant device is in use or under test:
- the collapse of, or the failure of any load-bearing part of, any amusement device provided as part of the fun fair which was designed to allow passengers to move or ride on it or inside it, or
- the failure of any safety arrangement connected with such a device, which is designed to restrain or support passengers.

(p) *Pipeline*. Either of the two following incidents in relation to a pipeline as defined by the Pipe Lines Act 1962:
- the bursting, explosion or collapse of a pipeline or any part thereof, or
- the unintentional ignition of anything in a pipeline, or of anything which immediately before it was ignited was in the pipeline.

(q) *Pressure vessels*. Explosion, collapse or bursting of any closed vessel, including a boiler or boiler tube, in which the internal pressure was above or below atmospheric pressure, which might have been liable to cause the death of, or any of the injuries or conditions described as notifiable above to, any person, or which resulted in the stoppage of the plant involved for more than 24 hours.

The HSE has produced two booklets to act as a guide to the requirements of the Regulations. These are:

- HSE 11: Reporting an injury or a dangerous occurrence.
- HSE 17: Reporting a case of disease.

Records
Employers and self-employed persons must keep a record of

(a) any event which is required to be reported showing:

- the date and time of the accident or dangerous occurrence,
- the full name and occupation of the person affected and the nature of the injury or condition,

- the place where the accident or dangerous occurrence happened,
- a brief description of the circumstances;

(b) any case of disease required to be reported showing:
- the date of the diagnosis of the disease,
- the occupation of the person affected,
- the name or nature of the disease.

Health and safety legislation

Main Acts pertaining to the legislation
These are as follows,

- The Health and Safety at Work Act 1974
- The Occupiers' Liability Acts 1957 and 1984
- The Employers' Liability (Compulsory Insurance) Act 1969
- The Factories Act 1961
- The Offices, Shops and Railway Premises Act 1963
- The Fire Precautions Act 1971.

Employers should be aware of these instruments and their responsibilities thereunder. Copies of the Acts and explanatory guides may be obtained from HMSO bookshops and accredited agents.

Health and safety regulations
Hundreds of separate regulations have been made under the various enactments since the commencement of HASAWA 1974; information about the regulations applying to particular industries is available from regional offices of the Health and Safety Executive (HSE). Regulations range from Asbestos (Licensing) Regulations 1983 to Young Persons (Employment) Order 1938.

Health and safety codes of practice
The Health and Safety Commission approves and issues codes of practice which provide practical guidance on any of the general duties specified in HASAWA 1974 or on health and safety requirements, or on any of the existing statutory provisions.

Failure to observe a code is not itself a ground for civil proceedings. However, in criminal proceedings, if there was an approved code of practice at the time the alleged offence was committed, failure to observe it will be taken into account by the Court. Examples of existing approved codes of practice are: Control of Lead at Work; Principles of Good Laboratory Practice; Safety Representatives and Safety Committees etc.

Health and safety guidance notes
While having no legal force, guidance notes and booklets issued by the HSC or the HSE contain practical advice on particular health and safety matters. Examples of these are: Accident Hazard Regulations 1984; Electric Headlamps; Occupational Health Services etc.

The HSE has recently published a booklet specifically aimed at smaller firms entitled 'Essentials of Health and Safety at Work'. This quality guide is available through HMSO Publications Centre, HMSO Bookshops and HMSO's accredited agents (see Yellow Pages under 'Booksellers').

7
Terminating Employment

There are two main ways in which the employment contract ends: either the employee gives notice, or you as the employer decide to terminate the employment of a particular member or members of your staff. There are a number of pitfalls for the unwary employer, but the first point to note is that if you have good cause for terminating the employment of a member of staff, and go about it in the correct way, there is no reason why you should be in a position where you have to defend 'unfair' dismissal proceedings at an industrial tribunal.

The employee gives notice

Any employee is entitled to give in his or her notice and should do so in the manner specified in the terms and conditions of employment. As we discussed in Chapter 2, it is best to ask for notice to be given in writing to a specified person so that there can be no misunderstandings later. The employee should give whatever period of notice is specified, eg one week or one month. This period allows you time to sort out all financial transactions relating to termination (for example holiday pay due or owing), and either to look for a replacement or reallocate duties among remaining members of staff.

Once you receive notice, you should agree with the employee the date on which he or she will actually leave the company. Should the employee be going to work for a competitor, and you would prefer immediate termination of employment (but the employee is willing to work the notice period) then you may by all means ask him or her to go; remember, however, that you are thereby stopping that individual from fulfilling his or her contract and you will still have to pay the balance of notice due – ie if your member of staff has to give you one month's notice, but you would prefer him or her to go that day, you must still pay the month's money which would otherwise be earned. Should your employee, however, ask to be released early, and you are happy to agree with that, then the earlier termination is by mutual agreement and the person should be paid only until the day of leaving your employ.

Do not try to coerce a person into accepting an earlier termination date in an attempt to save money during the notice period, because that could be construed as constructive dismissal notwithstanding the fact that your employee had already indicated a desire to leave.

Should your employee fail to give adequate notice, or no notice at all, what can you do? In practical terms, the answer is nothing. Although the employee is in breach of contract, unless you can prove material loss arising from the breach of contract (and you would have to pursue this through the courts), there is no compensation you are likely to be able to extract from the employee. If money is due to you from a loan or overpayment of holiday pay, you may be able to recoup this from any other money outstanding – it is sensible to allow for this in the terms of any loans made by the company. If your terms and conditions of employment say so, you might, in these circumstances, not pay any holiday money due. Otherwise the cost of taking a claim against an employee for breach of contract in failing to give notice will not be justified as you are unlikely to gain any financial recompense.

The only occasion when it may be worth pursuing an employee who fails to give notice is if he or she is not only in breach of notice requirements but has also gone to work for a competitor (in direct breach of another term of the contract) or has failed to return company documents or property as required by the terms and conditions. Return of property would usually be upheld by the courts (if the matter progressed that far); a restrictive covenant would be examined by the court and upheld if it was reasonable.

Can you refuse to accept a person's notice?
The answer is 'No'. You can try to persuade an employee not to resign and even offer inducements to stay (but be wary of doing this) but in the end everyone has a right to resign if they so wish, and if the person is adamant it is best to put a good face on it and make the best use of the notice period to ensure that he or she passes on to other employees the knowledge or skills which you are so reluctant to lose.

A change of mind

If employees change their minds after you have accepted their notice, do you have to allow them to continue with you? Again the answer is 'No'. Once notice has been given and accepted it is binding, and even if employees have a change of mind, you do not have to agree. You may do so, of course, if you did not want to lose them anyway, but there is no compulsion to do so. You should also remember that if you have already filled the post from internal sources, changing your mind could disappoint someone else who may be equally important to you; if you have recruited externally, you now have a contract with a third party who would be entitled to notice or payment in lieu of notice if you were to withdraw an offer of employment which has been accepted.

Exit interviews

When an employee resigns, it is sensible to talk to him or her and try to find out:

- why he or she decided to look elsewhere for a job;
- where he or she is going and the job being taken up;
- what he or she would like to say about the job – this can be useful information to feed into the selection process.

It is also sensible to put a note on the employee's file summarising the exit interview and also making a brief assesment of that person in case he or she applies to you again or you are asked for a reference. The same applies, of course, if you dismiss someone.

When the employer wishes to terminate employment

The law allows you five 'fair' reasons for terminating employment:

- lack of capability or lack of qualifications,
- conduct,
- redundancy,
- contravention of some other statutory enactment,
- 'some other substantial reason'.

If your reason for terminating employment falls into one of these categories, *and* termination has taken place in accordance with your own disciplinary rules or other agreements (as in the case of redundancy, for instance), there should be no case for you to answer at an industrial tribunal. You must, of course, make sure that there is no suggestion of sex or race discrimination in the reason for dismissal or in your choice of employees who are to be made redundant. You should also remember that the purpose of a disciplinary code is first and foremost, according to the ACAS Code of Practice No 1 'Disciplinary Practice and Procedures in Employment', to help the individual to reach the standards you expect, not to punish for failure to achieve.

Giving notice

You should give the employee or employees you wish to dismiss proper notice (unless dismissal is for gross misconduct and your disciplinary procedure allows you to dismiss without notice or pay in lieu of notice), 'proper' being what they are entitled to receive under their written terms and conditions of employment. In some circumstances you may wish the employees to leave at once, and would be prepared to pay them money in lieu of notice. However, as mentioned in Chapter 2, employees have the right to a period of notice, and you cannot insist on money in lieu. Should they refuse to accept such an offer, but you do not wish them to remain on the premises, the simplest recourse is to give the appropriate period of notice but tell them that you do not wish them to report for work or to visit the premises during that period, making payment as normal. If you are faced with a number of redundancies, and you recognise an independent trade union, there are certain other steps you must take to notify and inform the trade union and the Department of Employment. These are discussed later under 'Dismissal for redundancy' (see page 137).

Before dismissing someone, you should be clear as to the reasons for the dismissal and sure in your own mind what you are doing falls within the range of actions permitted by your own disciplinary code. You should also feel sure that the dismissal will not be seen as victimisation (that is, you have previously not dismissed others who have been guilty of the same or similar offences).

A disciplinary procedure will normally have an appeal mechanism built into it, and at the time of dismissal you should remind the employee of the right of appeal against the decision. The effective date of dismissal, if it is upheld, will normally be the date on which the dismissal takes place, not the date of the appeal. There is no reason, if dismissal is to take place with immediate effect, why the person should remain on the premises. He or she can be permitted to return for the appeal hearing.

The right to go to an industrial tribunal

A person who has been employed by you for two years or more, and works for more than 16 hours per week (or has worked for you for between 8 and 16 hours per week for 5 years or more) may dispute through an industrial tribunal your decision on dismissal. This is a statutory right and one which you cannot ask the employee to sign away except in one circumstance. That arises where a conciliation officer of ACAS is involved in the negotiations which end in dismissal on agreed terms, one of which may be that the employee relinquishes his or her right to proceed to an industrial tribunal and completes and signs form COT3. No other form of agreement is legally binding on the employee. The industrial tribunal procedure is described on pages 149–152.

Dismissal for lack of capability or lack of qualifications

Lack of capability

If you wish to dismiss an employee on these grounds you should be able to demonstrate that, despite the efforts you have made to help the employee to improve his or her work performance, the tasks reasonably expected are still not being carried out at a standard which is acceptable to you. Normally this shortfall will be caused by a basic inability or unwillingness to do the work expected. Occasionally, lack of capability may arise from genuine long-term sickness and this is discussed later in this section (see page 134).

To ensure that your dismissal for lack of capability is 'fair', you should be sure that the following steps have been taken:

- The shortfall in performance should have been discussed verbally with the person concerned and help offered in overcoming the problems, setting a date when performance will be reviewed. The length of time needed will depend on the complexity of the work and the degree of training or practice needed. For a simple repetitive task, this period might be fairly short – several days for instance. For a more complex clerical task, it might be two weeks. For a management or supervisory post, this period might be for one to three months.

- The verbal warning should have been followed up with a written warning if performance had not improved. This warning should have reiterated the standards you expected and the action taken to help the person concerned. Again, set a date when you will review performance. Make sure that you stick to that review date, that you have monitored performance constantly during the time under review and that you have carried out any action which you promised to take in terms of revision, further training etc.
- A final written warning should have been sent, after talking to the individual (if there is still no improvement in performance and you have done your best to help him or her), indicating that if the desired improvement has not taken place by a certain date, termination will follow.

If you recognise a trade union, it is customary to allow an employee to have his or her shop steward present at disciplinary hearings. If there is no trade union recognition, many companies suggest that if an employee wishes to be accompanied by a fellow employee this will be acceptable. In interviews to discuss lack of capability, as well those where the main issue is conduct, it is important to listen to what the employee has to say, not just to condemn him or her without hearing the reasons for a failure to reach the standards expected.

Cases of long-term sickness
It is recognised that there may be employees who are genuinely ill and may not be able to return to work in the foreseeable future. As long as termination is handled sympathetically and follows the rules of the company and those unwritten rules which a good employer would automatically follow, a tribunal is likely to allow that this is a 'fair' reason for dimissal. In order to ensure that you treat your employee in these circumstances as fairly as possible, you should follow these steps:

- maintain regular contact with the employee, visiting if possible;
- if employment is at risk, let the employee know;
- take medical advice, either from the employee's GP or from your own doctor if the terms and conditions of employment permit this;

- look for alternative work if the person could return to lighter duties;
- when it becomes impossible to keep the job open any longer, let the employee know that dismissal is imminent;
- if you have to dismiss, remember that the employee is entitled to his or her salary during the period of notice, even if unable to work. The period of notice must be that specified by statute or written terms and conditions, whichever is the longer.

The general rule is to be sympathetic, refrain from making premature judgements and get proper medical advice.

Lack of qualifications

There are few cases reaching tribunals where the 'fair' reason for dimissal is lack of qualifications. Generally, it is best to obtain evidence of qualifications before taking a person on. If the employment contract is in effect a training contract, it can normally be terminated at the end of the training period whether or not the person has successfully completed the required qualifications. It can be difficult to dismiss someone whom you had assumed possessed certain qualifications (or even claimed to have them), but did not, if that person had been doing the job to your satisfaction for a period of time. Tribunals will not be sympathetic unless you can prove that the lack of a qualification is a bar to continued employment because it prohibits you from offering certain services to the public. Tribunals may be equally unsympathetic if you dismiss a person for failing an examination related to the particular employment if he or she could resit the examination within a reasonably short period and have a good chance of succeeding.

Dismissal for misconduct

Conduct at work

You have the right to determine the standards which you expect your employee to reach and maintain; these should be made known when employment starts, if not before. Matters which the company regards as misconduct should be illustrated in the disciplinary procedure or the staff handbook so that employees know what is expected of them and what cannot be tolerated. Such illustrations do not have to be exhaustive but should reflect your particular circumstances. For instance, breach of a 'no smoking' rule may be a minor offence which will attract a verbal reprimand on the first occasion in an office environment, but may be cause for 'instant' dismissal in the works of a chemical processing company. The degree of danger for the person and the safety of others are obvious factors here. The same tends to apply to fighting. Fighting near moving or dangerous machinery, or with weapons such as knives, tends to attract a severer penalty, including dismissal, than instances when personal safety is not so threatened.

Dishonesty is another difficult area for the employer. Precedents at the Employment Appeals Tribunal (EAT) have clarified the thinking of what action you may 'fairly' take. The EAT has indicated that if you genuinely believe someone to be guilty, that the evidence supports that belief and that you have made diligent enquiries to arrive at the truth, then if, after the proper disciplinary procedure, the decision to dismiss is made and upheld on appeal, it will normally be considered 'fair'. You do not need to have the degree of proof which a court of law would need to make a prosecution stick. This highlights one of the problem areas for employers – whether or not to involve the police. The difficulty is that if the police cannot find sufficient evidence, they will not bring a prosecution. If they are not prepared to prosecute it is difficult for you, the employer, to say that despite the lack of evidence you intend to dismiss. You may therefore have disrupted your workforce, pointed the finger of suspicion at someone and then be powerless to take action; equally, the person concerned may not have the opportunity to clear his or her character through the courts.

As with dismissal for capability, you should go through the disciplinary procedure with the employees concerned, helping to improve their conduct (eg get into work on time) or change their attitudes (eg discriminatory behaviour). If they cannot or will not change their behaviour, the warnings move from verbal to written and then to a final written warning followed, if there is still no change, by dismissal.

Unless conduct is such that 'instant' dismissal is justified, the person should be given a proper period of notice or payment in lieu of notice.

In applying your disciplinary rules, it is important not to set precedents which may be used against you at a later date. Unfortunately, this removes some of the flexibility from management, as 'giving a second chance' to someone you feel genuinely sorry for may be turned into 'custom and practice' by unscrupulous employees.

Conduct outside work
If you hear that an employee has spent the night at the police station or has been arrested on a drunk driving charge, your first reaction may be to dismiss. However, before you take such drastic action, you should consider if it is justified. If the person concerned is going to be remanded in custody for an uncertain but probably lengthy period, then that person may well become incapable of fulfilling his or her side of the employment contract and may be fairly dismissed through lack of capability. If the offence of which the employee is accused has a direct bearing on his or her employment, (eg your cashier is accused of stealing money), it may be that your confidence in that person's suitability to continue doing the work for which he or she was engaged is shattered and dismissal would normally be fair. It is important, however, not to leap to conclusions and if the employee is remanded on bail, dismissal before being found guilty might well be deemed unfair by an industrial tribunal.

Dismissal for redundancy

This will normally be considered fair as long as you abide by any 'contractual' terms you may have about selection for redundancy or, failing that, stick to the principal of 'last in, first out'. In making your selection for redundancy it is important not to discriminate indirectly against women (who tend to be the part-timers) or a particular ethnic group (who may, for example, work together in a particular shop or on a particular shift). If you recognise a trade union, you must give the officials of the trade union (who in most cases will be the shop stewards or perhaps the district officer) proper notice of impending redundancies *in writing* (see Chapter 5).

A redundancy situation arises when work diminishes so that you do not need as many people, or you move the work to another workplace which your present employees could not reasonably be expected to journey to. If you have a mobility clause in your terms and conditions of employment, you could, of course, insist on transfers; if the employees refused, you would not be liable to make redundancy payments.

Use of a trial period

If a person is to be made redundant because the need for his or her skills has diminished or disappeared, but there are other jobs available, the law permits you to offer a 'trial' period of four weeks during which the employee may try out the job (and you may assess competence) without losing entitlement to a redundancy payment. Should another suitable job be available and the employee turns it down, the right to a redundancy payment is forfeited. The alternative offer must, however, be reasonable – that is, be work of a similar nature and status to that which was previously being done. It would not, for instance, be reasonable to offer a skilled man a job washing dishes in the canteen. A tribunal would say that the gradient in skills and job demand was too steep. (If you are operating in an area of high unemployment, however, and the person concerned is at an age where difficulty in getting another post might be experienced, he or she might be happy to remain with you in a lower level job. You should not assume that such a transfer would be unacceptable – ask first.)

Redundancy pay

The amount of statutory redundancy payment varies with age and length of service and is calculated using the amount of 'a week's pay' currently in force – £172 from April 1989. (This notional amount means that if you pay someone £300 per week, your obligation is limited to £172. If your employee is earning £90 per week, of course, the lower figure prevails.) The Department of Employment publishes a useful table to help you to calculate the number of weeks of pay due and this is given below. In summary, each year of service:

- before the age of 18 does not count;
- between the ages of 18 and 22 attracts half a week's pay;
- between the ages of 22 and 41 attracts one week's pay;
- over 41, and below 59 for a woman or 64 for a man, attracts 1½ week's pay.

In the last year before retirement, the amount due decreases with every month of service. (There is an anomaly in the law at present which will be amended by future legislation, which is that you may not insist that a woman retires before a man would have to, but if she works beyond 60 she is not currently entitled to any redundancy payment were she to be dismissed at, say 62, although a man of that age would be so entitled.)

Other aspects of redundancy pay
The preceding paragraph refers to statutory rights only. There may be situations where a company pays more than the statutory minimum, particularly if:

- the contract of employment refers to a redundancy policy which is more generous than that of the State;
- there is an agreement with a recognised trade union about the basis on which redundancy pay will be calculated. A company and trade union may make a joint application to the Secretary of State for Employment for exclusion from the requirements of the Employment Protection Act if the collective agreement contains provisions which are at least as good as those required by law.

Most procedures, whether in individual contracts or a collective agreement, will include statutory rights as part of the total payable. A clause in an individual contract might read:
'If the company has to make you redundant, you will be entitled to two weeks' pay per year or part-year of service. Any payment due under this provision will include any right to statutory redundancy pay'.

Consultation with trade unions
If you recognise a trade union, you must consult its representatives before (notification must be *in writing*) redundancies take place. The time scale is:

- if 10–99 employees are to be made redundant, at least 30 days beforehand;
- if 100 or more workers are affected, at least 90 days beforehand.

The purpose of consultation is:

- to see if the union can suggest solutions acceptable to the company which might make redundancies unnecessary (eg short-time working);
- to agree the procedure for the redundancies.

If you fail to consult in time, you may be ordered to pay a *protective award* by an industrial tribunal. This in effect guarantees the wages of those who are made redundant for the period of consultation which should have taken place.

Notifying the Department of Employment/union
If you intend to make 10 or more workers redundant from one establishment within a relatively short period, you must notify the Department:

- at least 30 days beforehand if 10–99 workers are affected; or
- at least 90 days beforehand if 100 or more are affected.

This notification period is the same as that which you must give to an independent, recognised trade union. The requirement still remains even if you are not entitled to any rebate for the payment you make or if the leavers are all volunteers. Where large numbers are involved, the Department will normally be helpful in discussing other opportunities with your staff, even setting up a temporary office on your premises where this is possible.

Both the Department and the trade union must be notified in writing. The Department requires form HR1 to be completed. This can be obtained from any redundancy payments office. In theory there is a financial penalty of £2000 available to the Department should you fail to notify, or the amount of rebate may be reduced. The financial penalties are likely to be greater, however, if you recognise a union and fail to give proper notice, as members can then apply for a protective payment to an industrial tribunal. This in effect gives employees the same pay as they would have received had you given the appropriate notice.

Rebates
The right to a rebate on the redundancy payments made has now been phased out except for those companies which, together with any associated companies, employ fewer than 10 employees. This will also be phased out when the 1988 Employment Bill becomes law.

Time off to look for work
Employees who are redundant have the right to take paid time off work to look for employment or arrange training. There is no exact limit laid down, but industrial tribunals have suggested that up to two days per week would not be unreasonable.

Dismissal for some other statutory reason

There might be some instances where to continue to employ a person would put you in breach of the law. Obvious examples are to continue to employ as a driver someone who has lost his or her driving licence. When there is no other work available, it will normally be fair to dismiss the employee concerned. It is important to set clear precedents so that you treat in a similar way everybody who falls into this category; otherwise you may be held to have dismissed unfairly because of your normal custom and practice.

Dismissal for some other substantial reason

This is intended to cover things which do not fit neatly into the other categories but where it is clearly reasonable that the employer should be able to dismiss without facing a claim for unfair dismissal. Concern about a possible breach of confidentiality if your secretary's husband were to join a close competitor is an example of a situation where you might dismiss for this reason. Other illustrations include failure to obtain a fidelity bond, refusal to sign an undertaking not to compete, personality clashes between employees, and if your best customer were unwilling to accept a particular individual. Employers should beware, however, that is it not intended to allow them to dismiss on any pretext and the proper procedure should be followed in all cases. Tribunals will need to be sure that your behaviour is not capricious.

Automatically unfair dismissal

There are some circumstances where it is automatically unfair to dismiss a person. These are:

- trade union membership or activities, of non-membership of a trade union;
- under the transfer of undertakings legislation, when a transfer is the main reason (unless there is an economic or technical reason for dismissal);
- pregnancy;
- sex or race;
- a spent conviction under the Rehabilitation of Offenders Act.

For a woman to complain of dismissal because of pregnancy, or any person because of a spent conviction, he or she must have had two years' with the employer. To bring a case on trade union, sex or race grounds, there is *no minimum service qualification*.

Contract frustration

Frustration of the contract occurs where the performance of the contract becomes impossible, that is the employee is not able to fulfil his duties. The most common causes of frustration of contract are:

- illness, and
- imprisonment.

If frustration of contract is proved, it means that there is no case of unfair dismissal for the employer to answer.

If you believe that the contract has ended in frustration, but the employee believes otherwise and makes a claim for unfair dismissal, that employee will first have to prove that he or she was dismissed. In arriving at its conclusions, the tribunal will take a number of factors into account including:

- length of previous employment;
- what kind of job was involved;
- the cause of the 'frustrating' event;
- how long employment could otherwise have been expected to last;
- the need of the employer to have the work done;
- whether or not the employee has continued to be paid;
- the behaviour of the employer in relation to the employee and whether or not action has been taken to terminate the contract;
- whether it would be reasonable to expect the employer to wait any longer for the employee to return to work.

In cases of frustration due to *illness or accident*, it may be fairer to the employee to terminate employment rather than rely on frustration where it becomes apparent that he or she will not work again for a considerable time.

Where *imprisonment* is the cause, it may be wiser for the employer to terminate the employment contract. In either situation this removes potential ambiguities.

Other reasons for termination of employment

There are a number of other ways in which the employment contract may be terminated, including insolvency, death, retirement and fundamental breach of contract.

Insolvency

This in itself does not terminate the employment contract but winding up a company will do so. If an employee is dismissed as a consequence he or she is entitled to claim certain payments, including any amount which the employer is due to pay for the statutory minimum period of notice. If the business is acquired by a third party, the transfer of undertakings regulations may make a dismissal unfair.

Death of either party

The death of an employee will naturally terminate the contract of employment, although any outstanding payments will have to be calculated and paid to his or her estate, along with any rights the estate may have to insurance payment or pension.

The death of the employer may frustrate the contract unless similar or alternative employment is offered by a successor.

Retirement

The date at which retirement becomes effective should be clearly spelt out in the contract of employment. If you operate a company pension scheme, it may also indicate the age at which early retirement may be taken on grounds of ill-health.

Since November 1987 it has been unlawful, under the Sex Discrimination Act 1986, to insist that women and men retire at different ages. If, therefore, the company's normal retirement age is 60 for women and 65 for men, it will be discriminatory and unlawful to insist that a women retires at 60 should she choose not to. However, for the present, arrangements for pension do not have to be at the same.

Fundamental breach of contract

Where either the employer or employee behaves in such a way as to make it clear that he or she does not intend to be bound by the terms of the contract (ie repudiates the contract), the other party may take that as an indication that the employment contract has been broken.

Instances of employee repudiation of contract include:

- refusing to carry out a 'lawful' order (that is, one which it is reasonable to request under his or her contract);
- telling the employer that the job is no longer wanted and walking off the premises;
- failing to return to work after being subject to discipline;
- not being available for work;
- refusing to accept a collectively agreed change where this is provided for in the contract.

Although any of these may be a fundamental breach, you should not jump to conclusions and put a P45 form in the next post. A premature assumption that words or actions in the heat of the moment are intended to be binding may lead to claims of unfair dismissal. It is best to allow a 'cooling down' period, after which steps may be taken to end the contract formally.

Constructive dismissal

Where you as the employer repudiate the contract, this may lead to a claim of 'constructive dismissal' by the employee. Constructive dismissal is the term given where the employee resigns and claims that resignation was forced upon him or her by the behaviour of the employer who appears to be breaching the terms of the contract. When such a case goes before a tribunal, the onus is on the employee to prove that he or she was dismissed. If the tribunal agrees that dismissal did take place, it will then decide if the dismissal was fair or not.

End of a training contract

Where a contract is for a specific period and its purpose is to help the employee to gain skills, knowledge or qualification (as with an apprenticeship or articles in a professional office), there is not normally a right to employment when that contract ends. Failure to offer employment in these circumstances will not normally be counted as unfair dismissal.

If you are considering dismissal, but want to avoid a claim for unfair dismissal, it can be tempting to try to persuade an employee to accept a sum of money in return for a signed piece of paper promising not to take any further action. This is not legally binding unless agreement has been reached through the auspices of an ACAS conciliation officer. You cannot require an employee to sign away his or her legal right. In any case it is not good management practice to 'buy off' potential trouble because it can set precedents and raise expectations among other employees that, if dismissed for whatever reason, they only have to mention 'tribunal' and sums of money will be forthcoming.

Written reason for dismissal

Any employee who has six months' service (this will be increased to two years when the 1988 Employment Bill becomes law), and is dismissed has the right to ask for the reason for dismissal in writing. You must provide this within 14 days or the employee can go to a tribunal which will normally award two weeks' pay for your failure to do so. It is obviously important that what you write in such a letter agrees with what you said to the employee at the time and what you put on any form, eg DHSS benefit forms or industrial tribunal.

It is helpful, where dismissal takes place, to ensure that all witnesses, managers and supervisors whose evidence of actions helped to arrive at the decision, have put clearly down on paper what happened and why decisions were taken. Claims for unfair dismissal may arrive after other people have left the company, and recalling their testimony may not be easy.

Remedies for unfair dismissal

If an employee is found to be unfairly dismissed, the industrial tribunal has to consider what would be an appropriate response. In completing his or her original claim for unfair dismissal, the employee is asked what remedy is being sought,: reinstatement (back in the old job), re-engagement (back with the employer but in a different job), or financial compensation.

In deciding which remedy to apply, the tribunal will look at all the circumstances leading up to the dismissal and the wishes of the employee and employer. If you have taken on somebody else to do the job originally held by the dismissed employee, this will not be a material factor unless you can prove that the work is so critical you could not have continued to operate without somebody in that post.

Financial compensation

In most circumstances this is made up of two amounts:

- a basic award, and
- a compensatory award.

The amount which can be awarded is reviewed from time to time by the Secretary of State for Employment. In recent years this review has been in April and new rates are usually announced at the end of December to come into force in April. The limits apply to both the basic and compensatory awards.

Basic award

This is calculated in the same way as entitlement to redundancy payment. There is a statutory limit which from April 1989 is £5160 (30 weeks at £172 per week). Each year the maximum pay which counts as 'a week's pay' is determined by the Secretary of State. From April 1989 this is £172. If the person earns less, then that is the amount taken into account.

In most circumstances, an employee would expect to receive full entitlement under the basic element of the award. However, there is no automatic right to any portion of it and if the tribunal found the dismissal unfair but the employee largely to blame (eg he or she had behaved in such a way that dismissal was almost inevitable but the employer had perhaps acted outside his own procedures) the tribunal has the power to reduce the amount of compensation by up to 100 per cent.

Compensatory award

This amount is intended to be some recompense for losses incurred by an employee because of his or her dismissal. The maximum from April 1989 is £8925. The tribunal will consider:

- lost earnings between dismissal and hearing;
- estimated future losses (for example if the employee will be unemployed for some time, or has had to take a lower paid job);
- loss of pension rights and other benefits.

Again, the tribunal may reduce the award if the employee was largely or partly to blame for his or her dismissal or has refused to take up other reasonable offers of employment.

If you paid wages in lieu of notice, or made an ex gratia payment, this will normally be deducted from any award made.

In addition to the basic and compensatory awards, there may

be a further amount awarded if you fail to conform to a reinstatement or re-engagement order. This additional award will be:

- 13–26 weeks' pay (subject to statutory maximum, £172 from April 1989), the amount entirely at the discretion of the tribunal, or
- between 26 and 52 weeks' pay, if dismissal was found to be unfair on grounds of sex or racial discrimination, subject to statutory maximum.

If therefore you unfairly dismissed a woman earning £172 per week in her fifties, with 30 years' service, and the tribunal determined that sex discrimination was at the root, and you failed to comply with a reinstatement order, the award could be somewhere in the region of £23,000.

Basic award	£ 5,160
Compensatory award	£ 8,925
Additional award	£ 8,944
	£23,029

Dismissal because of trade union membership activities or non-membership of an employee in a closed shop.

Employees have a right to choose whether or not they belong to a trade union; even if you do not recognise any union for collective bargaining or representation rights, you must not try to stop your employees belonging to or taking part in trade union activities (at appropriate times, of course). Should you dismiss somebody and the tribunal decides that the root cause was his or her trade union membership, then not only is dismissal automatically unfair but the financial penalties for employers are severe when the employee has asked to be reinstated. Compensation consists of:

- a basic award as before, but subject to a minimum of £2520;
- a compensatory award, as before;
- a special award.

This special award, payable where reinstatement has been asked for, may be:

- 104 weeks' pay (not subject to statutory limits) with minimum compensation of £12,550 and a maximum of £25,040 where the tribunal does not order reinstatement, or
- 156 weeks' pay (not subject to statutory limits) with a minimum payment of £18,795 where the tribunal orders reinstatement but the employer fails to comply with the order.

Summary

Employers, who win the majority of unfair dismissal cases, do not have to tolerate unsatisfactory employees but, in order to ensure that dismissal is found to be fair, should:

- operate within the terms of their own disciplinary procedure;
- be consistent;
- treat such employees with consideration;
- ensure that the reason for dismissal falls within those categories deemed to be 'fair';
- be certain that dismissal is not because of sex, race or trade union membership.

Industrial tribunals

An industrial tribunal may be asked to adjudicate on a wide range of statutory employment provisions.

The Acts under which the tribunals may hear cases are:

Employment Protection (Consolidation) Act 1987
Employment Acts 1980, 1982, 1988
Equal Pay Act 1970
Equal Pay Amendment Regulations 1983
Sex Discrimination Acts 1975, 1986
Race Relations Act 1976
Wages Act 1986.

A tribunal may hear a claim initiated by:

- employers,
- an employee or ex-employee,
- a trade union or its officials.

Tribunal procedure

Originating notice of application
To initiate a hearing, the employee will begin by completing a form IT1 stating:

- his or her name and address,
- the employer's name and address,
- the grounds on which the tribunal is being asked to make a decision.

Time constraints
An individual has three months in which to make a claim (although tribunals have a certain discretion to hear a case outside the time limit where there are genuine reasons why the case could not be presented earlier), with the following exceptions:

- an ex-employee may make a claim for unfair dismissal up to six months after the date of dismissal if he or she was dismissed in a strike action;
- the time limit is six months where an employee is pursuing a claim for redundancy payment.

Respondent's 'notice of appearance'
The employer will receive a copy of the originating notice and has 14 days in which to 'enter an appearance'. A form for this purpose is obtainable from the tribunal office and requires the respondent to:

- set out his or her name and address;
- state whether it is intended to resist the application;
- if so, to set out on what grounds, giving sufficient information.

If the form is not returned within 14 days the right to appear to defend the case may be lost, although the employer may still be called as a witness and receive a copy of the decision. The employer may request an extension to the time limit if it is not practicable to respond within the 14 days. This notice of appearance indicates the intention to resist the claim.

Conciliation

The next step in most cases is for all the relevant papers to be sent to a conciliation officer of ACAS who will try to assist both parties to reach a settlement. If a settlement is reached the employee cannot re-open the case against the employer at a later stage. The settlement is legally binding, but a conciliation officer cannot prevent an individual from proceeding with a claim where no agreement is reached. The information given to the conciliation officer during his discussions is confidential and is not admissable in evidence at the tribunal hearing unless the person who provided the information agrees to it.

Disclosure

Either side in the case, or the tribunal itself, may request further information, more detail or relevant documents to be made available. Such documents might include:

- contracts of employment,
- notice of dismissal,
- time sheets,
- medical notes,
- performance appraisals, etc.

Confidentiality or public interest are not a defence to disclosure although a tribunal will vet the information before it makes it public. Documents prepared in conjunction with a conciliation officer will not be used. The only other exclusions are:

- where national security may be involved;
- where the collection of information requested would be excessive in terms of the value of that information.

Witnesses

The tribunal can order attendance if requested by either party and ask witnesses to produce documents. The witnesses may be questioned by either side.

Pre-hearing assessment

The tribunal, or either party, may request a pre-hearing assessment to try to prevent a waste of time and expense where it is felt that the case is so insubstantial that it is unlikely to succeed. These pre-hearing assessments are held before a full tribunal but witnesses are not called. The case will not be decided at this stage and the tribunal has no power to insist that the case does not proceed, although if the appellant does proceed against the opinion of the tribunal and loses at the full hearing he may have to pay costs.

Interim hearings
In cases of dismissal on grounds of trade union membership, an interim hearing may be held. This is designed to obtain an order that the employer should continue to employ the employee, or continue to pay him or her until the full hearing.

The hearing
Both parties should receive 14 days' notice of the time and place of the hearing. There are several points to note:

- This will normally be held in public; it is unusual for a tribunal to agree to a hearing in private.
- Either party may choose to send written representations and not attend, although these do not carry as much weight as a personal representation.
- Witnesses should be available for questioning by either party.
- If either party fails to attend, the tribunal must use the statements of the absent party and the case can be heard in their absence.
- Both parties are free to represent themselves or to be accompanied by another person or to be represented by the legal profession.
- Legal aid is not available.
- Evidence is taken on oath or affirmation but the proceedings are generally informal.
- Tribunals are not bound by precedent but will usually take account of decisions made by the Employment Appeals Tribunal and will be bound by judgements made by the Court of Appeal or the House of Lords.
- The employee will make his case first where the dismissal is in dispute (ie constructive dismissal), or the complaint is out of time, or he has less than two years' employment and is claiming an inadmissible reason for dismissal, or he is claiming sex or race discrimination. In other cases the employer will begin.

- Each side may cross-examine the other. Both sides have the right to address the tribunal.

The decision
A tribunal may make a majority decision, but where there is a dissenting member the reasons must be stated. The decision may be given at the end of the hearing, or the tribunal may reserve its decision and give it in writing at a later date. In any event each party will later be given written reasons for the decision.

Costs
Costs are not normally awarded as part of the tribunal decision unless:

- there was a pre-hearing assessment at which the appellant was advised not to proceed;
- the appellant or defendant has created unreasonable delays in continual postponements;
- a tribunal decides that a party 'has in bringing or conducting the proceedings acted unreasonably'.

Costs, if awarded, are on the County Court scale.

Appeals
Appeal may be made from an industrial tribunal decision, on points of law only, to the Employment Appeal Tribunal. The appeal must be sent within 42 days of the date on which the decision was sent, stating the point of law on which the appeal is based.

The Employment Appeal Tribunal (EAT)

Constitution
The EAT consists of three people: the chairman (who is a Judge of the High Court), and two lay members appointed after consultation with the Confederation of British Industry, the Trades Union Congress, and other interested employers' or employees' associations.

Jurisdiction
The EAT may hear a point of law arising from a tribunal case which may be where:

- a tribunal has misdirected itself or misunderstood the law;
- a tribunal has misunderstood or misapplied the facts;
- there has been a breach of the rules of natural justice.

Powers of the EAT
These are similar to those of an industrial tribunal.

Costs
The EAT will not usually award costs, but they may be included in an award for the late withdrawal of an appeal.

Appeals
On a point of law, an appeal may be made to the Court of Appeal (or the Court of Session in Scotland). Further appeal may be made from the Court of Appeal to the House of Lords.

8
Government Bodies and Employment

This chapter considers the main institutions which influence the management of people and relationships between employer and employee. The mainspring of these is outlined below.

The Department of Employment

This operates throughout the United Kingdom with the exception of Northern Ireland and is run by the Secretary of State for Employment and his staff. It has a number of broad responsibilities, arising from government policy, to fulfil:

- national and regional manpower policy;
- promotion of equal employment opportunities;
- payment of unemployment and (where applicable) supplementary benefits to eligible members of the population.

The department is also charged with the following industrial relations responsibilities:

- overview and administration of wages councils, industrial tribunals, and the Employment Appeal Tribunal (EAT);
- courts of enquiry;
- administration of most employment legislation.

The department collects and publishes a wide variety of labour and economic statistics, including numbers employed/unemployed, by region, by industrial sector; retail price movements (RPI and TPI). This information appears monthly in the *Department of Employment Gazette*. It also supplies earning surveys, an annual census of employment and an annual summary of wage rates and hours worked in the UK. All the main figures and movements are collated in the annual *Year Book of Labour Statistics*.

Advisory, Conciliation and Arbitration Service (ACAS)

On January 1976, arising from the Employment Protection Act 1975, an independent statutory body was set up to promote better industrial relations and to foster the extension of collective bargaining within the nation. This body is ACAS, which is very well known and has enjoyed some notable success in both its charges.

ACAS is governed by a ten-person council consisting of a full-time chairman and nine others, all appointed by the Secretary of State for Employment. Three members are recommended by the Confederation of British Industry (CBI) and three by the Trades Union Congress (TUC). Additional members may be appointed by the Secretary of State should the need arise. ACAS covers a range of activities:

- enquiring into any industrial relations matters with the consent of the parties concerned;
- providing advice on industrial relations and the development of effective personnel practices;
- producing codes of practice offering practical guidance towards better industrial relations;
- helping to resolve industrial disputes using conciliation, arbitration, mediation or committees of investigation as may be appropriate;
- resolving disputes over statutory employment rights between individual employees and their employers;
- carrying out enquiries into Wages Councils if requested by the Secretary of State for Employment.

ACAS may provide advice, where requested, in a number of ways:

- answering questions on how to interpret employment legislation;
- short advisory visits;
- in-depth assistance either to advise on a particular project or to identify the causes of more rooted problems and recommend means to solve them, working with management and unions jointly;
- organising training seminars and other courses.

Industrial tribunals

Where the efforts of ACAS may prove to be of no avail, a dispute between employee(s) and employer may be referred to an industrial tribunal. These were originally established under the Industrial Training Act 1964 to hear appeals by employers against training levy assessments. They now have jurisdiction in many areas dealing with individual rights arising under employment legislation, for example:

- Employment Acts 1980, 1982
- Employment Protection Act 1975
- Employment Protection (Consolidation) Act 1978
- Equal Pay Act 1970
- Equal Pay (Amendment) Regulations 1983
- Race Relations Act 1976
- Sex Discrimination Acts 1975, 1986
- Transfer of Undertakings Regulations 1982
- Wages Act 1986

Industrial tribunals are independent judicial bodies, each having a legally qualified chairman appointed by the Lord Chancellor (Lord President in Scotland). Each tribunal is composed of three members, the other two being drawn from panels of members appointed by the Secretary of State for Employment after consultation with the CBI and TUC.

In most cases placed before a tribunal, copies of documents and other written evidence are sent to an ACAS conciliation officer who will try to help the two parties to reach a settlement. (In addition, since October 1980, a pre-hearing assessment may be held in order to examine the dispute. The tribunal, having heard details, may advise an appellant not to proceed. The appellant does not have to heed this advice and can decide to progress the case to a full hearing by the tribunal.) If a conciliated settlement is not achieved, a hearing occurs before the tribunal, at which the employer and employee may make representations either personally or through an individual of their choice. A tribunal decision may result in one party paying the other a cash award or, in substantiated unfair dismissal cases, an order for reinstatement or re-engagement of the appellant.

Employment Appeal Tribunal (EAT)

There is a right of appeal by either party to the Employment Appeal Tribunal on points of law. The EAT is a superior court of record, an appellate body dealing with questions of law arising from industrial tribunals. The EAT also hears appeals on questions of law or fact arising from the decisions and activities of the Certification Officer (see page 163), and on complaints of unreasonable exclusion from trade union membership (Employment Act 1980). This body consists of judges and other members who have industrial relations experience. The judges are nominated by the Lord Chancellor from among High Court Judges and by the Lord President of the Court of Session (Scotland) from among Judges of that Court. The lay members have relevant experience as employer or employee representatives and are appointed on the joint recommendation of the Lord Chancellor and the Secretary of State for Employment.

There are further stages of appeal available, namely the Court of Appeal and, given permission, the House of Lords. It is also possible for an appellant in certain circumstances to present a case before the European Court of Justice relying on EC law.

The Central Arbitration Committee (CAC)

Another body to which, with the agreement of both parties, ACAS can refer an issue for voluntary arbitration is the Central Arbitration Committee. This was established by the Employment Protection Act 1975 (Schedule 1) which sets out its constitution and proceedings. It came into operation in February 1976. The chairman, deputy chairman and members are appointed by the Secretary of State for Employment, the members having experience as representatives of employers or employees. Except at informal hearings, a case will normally be heard by a chairman and a member from each side of industry. The chairman has the powers of umpire. The CAC provides both voluntary and unilateral arbitration. In the latter instance, the cases involve disclosure of information. The CAC also determines references made to it under the Equal Pay Act 1970 and several Acts which carry a fair wages clause (eg Independent Broadcasting Act 1973). As the Fair Wages Resolution itself has been repealed, the CAC no longer has to consider such matters.

The Health and Safety Commission and the Health and Safety Executive

The continuing need to secure the health, safety and welfare of people at work and other third parties was highlighted by the Health and Safety at Work Act (HASAWA) 1974. This Act was designed to give industrial safety a new impetus by underlining the joint and separate responsibilities of employer and employee. It took the form of enabling legislation, gathering to itself the individual orders and parts of safety law within the United Kingdom. The Health and Safety Commission and the Health and Safety Executive were established to further the purposes of the Act.

The *Commission* is charged with carrying out research, providing advice on health and safety matters and making any appropriate regulations. The *Executive* carries out the directives of the commission.

The Training Agency

The Employment Act 1988 established a body with responsibility to help people to train for employment commensurate with their ages and capabilities. It was also charged with seeking means to improve further training systems and methods, and is now known as the Training Agency. Formerly the Training Commission and, prior to that, the Manpower Services Commission, the Agency, which is part of the Department of Employment, is responsible to the Secretary of State. Since the trade unions decided not to support the government's Employment Training (ET) initiative, the Agency has lost its Commission status. The Training Commission itself, whose sole remaining function is the overseeing of Industrial Training Boards (see page 159) will be formally wound up through legislation in the next session of Parliament.

The Agency has two divisions: the Vocational Education and Training Group and the Skills Training Agency. The former has responsibility for promoting effective training activities to meet the manpower needs of the nation. It works with industry but adheres to the tenet that the responsibility for training rests with industry itself. The latter provides a network of skill centres and a team of mobile instructors to provide a highly flexible training service wherever needs arise, and with the emphasis on new technology.

The aims of the Agency are:

- fostering the modernisation of occupational training schemes;
- improving the skills of the unemployed better to equip them for employment;
- broadening the opportunities for adults to train and retrain;
- providing foundation and vocational training for young people under 18;
- assisting disadvantaged groups to receive appropriate training;
- enhancing the commitment of employers to training.

Industrial Training Boards (ITBs)

The Industrial Training Act 1964, enables the Secretary of State for Employment to establish Industrial Training Boards (ITBs) by industrial training orders. He appoints the chairman and board members, the intention being to promote training of people above school leaving age for employment in industry and commerce.

These Boards are empowered to:

- provide training and the necessary facilities for people employed in the industry or intending to be so employed;
- vet and approve courses and facilities provided by third parties;
- make recommendations concerning training for specific tasks and any associated further education needed for success, the standards to be achieved, and the means of assessing results;
- apply selection tests and other tests and methods for examining purposes, and to award certificates of competence as appropriate;
- provide help in finding facilities for being trained for employment in the industry;
- foster and carry out research into any matter relating to training for employment in the industry;
- provide advice about training relevant to the industry.

Under the 1964 Act (Section 2), an ITB may pay maintenance and travelling allowances to persons attending approved courses. It can make grants or loans to persons providing training courses and pay fees to persons providing further education for courses provided or approved by the Board.

ITBs may require employers in their respective industries to submit returns and other information, and to keep records for the purposes of the Act (Section 6).

The ITBs are financed by levies on employers in the industries which the particular Boards serve (Section 4). There is a right of appeal to an industrial tribunal against a levy by an ITB (Section 12). Exemption from levy payments may be granted by ITBs to employers who make their own training arrangements provided they are deemed to be adequate and are being implemented (Sections 4a and 4b).

There are only eight ITBs in existence (including the Agricultural Training Board). These cover:

- Clothing and allied products
- Construction
- Engineering
- Hotel and catering
- Offshore petroleum
- Plastic processing
- Road transport.

The 1964 Act has been amended by the Employment and Training Act 1981, authorising the Secretary of State for Employment to amend or revoke an industrial training order. This enables the Secretary of State to establish, alter or abolish an ITB following consultation with the Training Agency, whose advice he is not bound to heed.

The Equal Opportunities Commission (EOC) and the Commission for Racial Equality (CRE)

These Commissions were established under the Sex Discrimination Act 1975 and the Race Relations Act 1976.

Equal Opportunities Commission
The Equal Opportunities Commission has the following duties and responsibilites:

- to work towards the elimination of discrimination;
- to promote equal opportunity between men and women generally;
- to review the working of the Act, the Equal Pay Act 1970 and the Equal Pay (Amendment) Regulations 1983.

Commission for Racial Equality
The Commission for Racial Equality replaces the old Race Relations Board and is charged with:

- working towards the elimination of discrimination;
- promoting equality of opportunity and good relations between people of different racial groups;
- reviewing the working of the Act.

The EOC and the CRE were established by their respective Acts as independent bodies whose members are appointed by the Secretary of State for Employment. There are many functions within their remit.

- They can conduct formal investigations and compel disclosure of information for this purpose. They will prepare a formal report which may or may not be published. However, enquiries must not be too wide and there must be grounds for investigation (ie 'fishing trips' are not permitted).
- They can issue non-discrimination notices relating to discriminatory acts, practices, advertisements and instructions or pressure to discriminate. The notices forbid the act in question and may require the employer concerned to inform the relevant Commission (and any other interested parties, eg a recognised independent trade union) of the change made to remove the unlawful act. The hearing by the respective Commission to decide whether a notice should be issued is administrative and the information on which it is acting in issuing a non-discrimination notice must be disclosed to the employer involved. Appeals against such notices relating to employment are heard by an industrial tribunal. A register of these notices is kept and is open to public inspection. The Commissions may subsequently make enquiries to ensure compliance with the order.
- They can deal with persistent discrimination. In these cases, the relevant Commission can apply to a designated County Court for an injunction.
- They can bring an action in an industrial tribunal in cases of discriminatory advertisements, recruitment and employment practices, instructions or pressure to discriminate.
- They can help aggrieved persons to decide whether or not to proceed. This may include posing written questions to the

potential respondent, the answers to which (or failure to answer) will be admissible evidence if the complaint progresses.
- In special cases (test cases) the relevant Commission may give advice, help settlement, provide legal advice and arrange for representation.

Codes of Practice
Both Commissions have published codes of practice on employment which employers are expected to follow. These cover all aspects of employment and employers are required to review their practices and procedures regularly to ensure that they conform to the requirements of the law.

The Data Protection Registrar

Under the Data Protection Act 1984, employers who are data users and employees who are data subjects have obligations and rights. To ensure that these are properly fulfilled, the Act allows for the appointment of the Data Protection Registrar.

All companies who use mechanical or computerised data to maintain employee records are likely to be data users in the terms of the Act and must therefore register as such with the Registrar. Should this officer refuse an application to register, he must give his reasons for rejection to the company applying and inform them of their right to appeal, within 28 days, to the Data Protection Tribunal. (Appeals against the findings of this tribunal must be on a point of law and go to the High Court (Court of Session in Scotland).)

The prime duty of the Registrar is to promote obervance of the designated data protection principles by data users and persons carrying on computer bureaux. In addition, he is responsible for:

- maintenance of the register;
- investigation of any complaints (which may lead to a need for remedial action, namely an enforcement notice demanding compliance with the Act, a search and examine notice (of the data users' premises), a deregistration notice, a transfer prohibition notice (to stop transfer of personal data outside the United Kingdom) and finally court proceedings;
- communication with the public;
- advice to individuals;

- encouragement, through trade associations etc, of codes of practice for data users;
- preparation of an annual report to be laid before each House of Parliament.

Failure to comply with the requirements of the Data Protection Act 1984 is an offence which may give rise to criminal proceedings instituted by the Registrar or by or with the consent of the Director of Public Prosecution. Upon conviction, the offending company (an individual can be co-joined) may be fined (unlimited) and ordered to correct or erase any incorrect personal data. The courts may order compensation to be paid by the data user for damage and any associated distress suffered by a data subject due to loss of data; destruction of data without the authority of the data user; inaccurate data. Where data are shown to be inaccurate, the court may require correction or erasure of the data and any recorded conclusions based upon them. In certain instances, the court may decide that the true facts be inserted without erasure of the inaccuracy. Where a data subject has been damaged by leakage of personal data and there is a strong risk that such leakage could recur, the court may order erasure. Where a computer bureau is involved, all efforts would be made to allow the data user to remove the data to his keeping.

The Act does not apply to handwritten or typewritten staff records. However, if computerised data is later transferred to manual files, the data user will have to register. Manually prepared and maintained personnel records may be continued without any right of access by employees.

Certification Officer

Under the Employment Protection Act 1975, this officer is appointed by the Secretary of State for Employment. He may call upon support services from ACAS but is independent of that body and the Department of Employment. His work is concerned with trade unions and employers' associations. Among his many duties is that of listing trade unions and subsequently issuing certificates of independence to them where justified. It is possible that an employer may come in contact with this officer as part of an enquiry into the independent status (or otherwise) of a trade union which represents the employer's staff and/or manual workers.

Since 1980, the Certification Officer is empowered to refund certain expenditure incurred by independent trade unions in conducting postal ballots.

Wages Councils

These are statutory bodies established under the Wages Council Act 1979 and the Wages Act (Part II) 1986. Under the latter Act, young persons (under 21) have been removed from the scope of the Councils. The main function of a Wages Council is making an order which:

- fixes a single minimum hourly rate of remuneration in respect of all the time worked by an employee in any one week;
- sets:
  — a single minimum hourly rate of remuneration in respect of the basic hours worked by an employee in any one week,
  — a single minimum hourly overtime rate in respect of time worked in excess of the basic hours in any week by the employee;
- fixes a limit to any deductions from pay or charges imposed by an employer for providing an employee with living accommodation.

All other terms and conditions of employment are determined directly between the employer and employee.

There are approximately 26 Wages Councils which cover industries ranging from aerated waters, to laundry, to unlicensed places of refreshment. In addition, there is the Agricultural Wages Board. Under the 1986 Wages Act, the Secretary of State for Employment can at any time make an order varying the powers of any Wages Council or abolishing it from a specified date.

The government is actively considering the abolition of the Wages Councils.

Initiatives for dealing with unemployment

There are a number of initiatives begun by the government to help deal with the problems of unemployment. These are subject to change, and readers who might wish to make use of them are advised to check the details first.

Employment training

Employment training (or ET as it has become known) is the latest government initiative and is designed particularly to help the long-term unemployed. This was the provision which failed to get support from the TUC at its September 1988 conference and thus led to the early demise of the Training Commission. It replaces the Community Programme and the old and new Job Training Programmes.

Employment training is available to anyone who has been unemployed for over six months, though priority is given to those between 18 and 24 who have been unemployed for more than six but less than twelve months, and to those aged 18–50 who have been out of work for more than two years. It is intended to be a mix of practical and off-the-job training. Those who wish to participate will be assessed by a Training Agent who will agree a personal action plan with the individual and place him or her with a Training Manager who will see the programme through.

Youth Training Scheme

The Youth Training Scheme (or YTS) is open to all 16- and 17-year-olds leaving school, and to disabled people up to the age of 21. The scheme offers an opportunity to gain a recognised vocational qualification by means of on- and off-the-job training. YTS is organised through Managing Agents who have to be approved.

Job Splitting Scheme

The Job Splitting Scheme offers a government grant of £840 to employers for each full-time job which is split. To be eligible for the grant, the existing job must have been held by a full-time employee for at least three months immediately prior to the application. The job must be split into two part-time jobs and the newly created part-time jobs must be filled by people who are genuinely unemployed, or under threat of redundancy, or coming to the end of a YTS placement. The job must remain split for at least one year. The last part of the grant is not payable until the end of 12 months.

Appendices

Appendix 1
Forms Required by Law

Itemised pay statement

Employees who work for you for 16 hours a week or more, or who have worked for you between 8 and 16 hours per week for 5 years or more, are entitled to an itemised pay statement which must include:

- gross wages/salary;
- net wages/salary;
- fixed and variable deductions and why they are made;
- the amount and method of each payment where parts of the net amount are paid in different ways.

National Insurance contributions (NIC)

The amount of NIC depends on:

- whether or not the employee is contracted into the State pension scheme;
- the level of individual earnings.

Rates are usually revised by the Chancellor of the Exchequer in his Budget. Most employees fall within Category A (over 16 and under pensionable age) although some women may still pay the reduced rate (category B) and others may not make a contribution because, although still employed, they are over State pensionable age. 1988–89 rates are shown overleaf.

Weekly earnings	Not contracted out		Contracted out	
	employee	employer	employee	employer
Up to £40.99	no liability		no liability	
£41.00–£69.99	5%	5%	3%	1.20%
£70.00–£104.99	7%	7%	5%	3.20%
£105.00–£154.99	9%	9%	7%	5.20%
£155.00–£305.00	9%	10.45%	7%	6.65%
More than £305.00	No further liability	10.45% on all earnings	9% on first £41 7% on £41–305	10.54% on first £41 6.65% on £41–305 10.45% on balance

The percentage rates apply to all earnings where income falls within a particular band.

Class 2 (self-employed)

	£
Rate per week	4.05
Annual earnings exception limit	2,250

Class 3 (voluntary)

	£
Rate per week	3.95

Class 4 (self-employed)

Rate	6.30%

	£
Lower annual limit	4,750
Upper annual limit	15,860

The employer collects the employees' NIC by deducting it from salary and then paying both his and the employees' contributions to the Inland Revenue within 14 days of the end of the income tax month. This can be incorporated with the PAYE returns but both must be shown separately on the employees' pay slips.

Statutory sick pay (SSP)

Records must be kept for a minimum of three years detailing:

- dates of each period of incapacity for work (PIW)
- agreed qualifying days;
- SSP payments made to each employee in weekly, monthly and yearly figures;
- dates when SSP was not paid (and the reasons);
- leavers' statements issued and received by the employer;
- annual figures for gross SSP paid to each employee and to all employees in total (Form P11 – deductions working sheet).

To reclaim SSP, employers may deduct the gross amount paid from the total of the employees' and employer's Class 1 NIC for the tax month in which SSP has been paid. If the amount of SSP paid is greater then NIC, the remainder can be reclaimed by deducting it from PAYE due.

To recompense employers for the administrative effort this requires, they may reclaim 7 per cent of all SSP payments made for the year by deducting the amount from NIC payments which are due in any tax month after the SSP has been paid.

Form SSP1(L) must be issued to any leaver who has had a PIW within the eight weeks leading up to the last day of employment, if SSP was payable during that period for at least one week. (This is to allow a new employer to take account of any PIW if the employee falls ill within the first 8 weeks of employment.) Form SSP(T) is to be given to employees who are about to exhaust their 28 weeks' entitlement no later than the 23rd week of sickness.

Statutory maternity pay

The employer must keep the following records for at least three years:

- dates of absence as notified by the employee and actual dates if these are different;

- weeks in which SMP was paid and details of how much;
- weeks when SMP was not paid and the reasons;
- maternity or other medical certificates provided by employees for whom SMP is payable.

SMP is reclaimed in the same way as SSP.

Drivers' hours

Anyone who drives a vehicle in excess of 3½ tonnes gross weight (including trailers) in the UK or EEC is bound by certain rules. Their observance should be monitored by a tachograph fitted into the vehicle, which records all hours of work, rest periods and distances travelled. The employer must keep records and monitor them to ensure observance of the rules. Rules relating to hours are:

- no more than 9 hours' total driving daily (may be up to 10 hours on not more than 2 days per week);
- no more than 6 consecutive daily driving periods before a weekly rest period;
- no more than 90 hours' driving time per fortnight;
- a break to be taken after 4½ hours' driving time;
- breaks after 4½ hours to be at least 45 minutes (or 3 × 15 minutes during or immediately after the period);
- at least 11 consecutive hours' rest during each 24-hour period (there is some flexibility here);
- where there are two drivers each must have a rest period of a minimum of 8 consecutive hours in any period of 30 hours;
- weekly rest periods must total a minimum of 45 consecutive hours (again some flexibility). Reduced rest periods must be made good within 3 weeks by the deficit being taken en bloc. (A week is defined as 00.00 Monday to 24.00 Sunday.)

Accidents

Form F2508 must be used to report any fatal accident, major injury/condition or dangerous occurence. This is the written notification which should follow a telephoned notification. (See also Chapter 6, page 121.)

Registered disabled persons

An annual return must be completed giving details of all

registered disabled people you employ. (See also Chapter 1, page 29.)

Employing young persons

There are records which must be kept if employment is in a factory. (See also Chapter 1, page 34)

Appendix 2
Recommended Reading

The Advisory, Conciliation and Arbitration Service has published a series of booklets which are useful introductions to their subject. They are available from ACAS offices and cover the following topics:

No 1 Job evaluation
No 2 Introduction to payment systems
No 3 Personnel records
No 4 Labour turnover
No 5 Absence
No 6 Recruitment and selection
No 7 Induction of new employees
No 8 Workplace communications
No 9 The company handbook
No 10 Employment policies
Employing people: The ACAS handbook for small firms
Discipline at work: the ACAS advisory handbook

ACAS also publishes three codes of practice which employers are expected to observe:

- Disciplinary practice and procedures in employment
- Disclosure of information to trade unions for collective bargaining purposes
- Time off for trade union duties and activities

Codes of practice are available from HMSO.

The Department of Employment also publishes some useful booklets. The series includes:

No	1	Written statement of main terms and conditions of employment
No	2	Procedure for handling redundancies
No	3	Employees' rights on insolvency of employer
No	4	Employment rights for the expectant mother
No	5	Suspension on medical grounds under health and safety regulations
No	6	Facing redundancy? – Time off for job hunting or to arrange training
No	7	Union membership rights and the closed shop including the union labour only provisions of the Employment Act 1982
No	8	Itemised pay statement
No	9	Guarantee payments
No	10	Employment rights on the transfer of an undertaking
No	11	Rules governing continuous employment and a week's pay
No	12	Time off for public duties
No	13	Unfairly dismissed?
No	14	Rights on termination of employment
No	15	Union secret ballots
No	16	Redundancy payments

Further Reading from Kogan Page

Don't Do. Delegate! James N Jenks and John M Kelly
Effective Interviewing, John Fletcher
Effective Performance Appraisals, Robert B Maddux
Executive Survival: A Guide to Your Legal Rights, Martin Edwards
Getting the Best Out of People, David Robinson
Law for the Small Business, 6th edition, Patricia Clayton
Readymade Interview Questions, Malcolm Peel
Team Building, Robert B Maddux

Appendix 3
Useful Addresses

Advisory, Conciliation and Arbitration Service (ACAS)

Head Office:
27 Wilton Street
London SW1X 7AZ
01-210 3000

London and South East Region:
Clifton House
83–117 Euston Road
London NW1 2RB
01-388 5100

South West Region:
Regent House
27a Regent Street
Clifton
Bristol BS8 4HR
0272 744066

Midlands Region:
Alpha Tower
Suffolk Street
Queensway
Birmingham B1 1TZ
021-631 3434

66 Houndsgate
Nottingham NG1 6BA
0602 415450

Northern Region:
Westgate House
Westgate Road
Newcastle upon Tyne NE1 1TJ
091-261 2191

Yorkshire and Humberside Region:
Commerce House
St Albans Place
Leeds LS2 8HH
0532 431371

North West Region:
Boulton House
17–21 Chorlton House
Manchester M1 3HY
061-228 3222

249 St Mary's Road
Garston
Liverpool L19 0NF
051-427 8881

Scotland
Franborough House
123 Bothwell Street
Glasgow G2 7JR
041-204 2677

Wales:
Phase 1
Ty Glas Road
Llanishen
Cardiff CF4 5PH
0222 762636

Agricultural Wages Board
Eagle House
90–96 Cannon Street
London EC4N 6HT
01-623 4266

Central Arbitration Committee
39 Grosvenor Place
London SW1X 7BD
01-210 3738

Certification Officer
27 Wilton Street
London SW1X 7AZ
01-210 3734

Commission for Racial Equality
Elliot House
10–12 Allington Street
London SW1E 5EH
01-828 7022

Data Protection Registrar
Springfield House
Water Lane
Wilmslow
Cheshire SK9 5AX
0625 535711

Department of Employment
Head Office:
Caxton House
Tothill Street
London SW1H 9NF
01-273 6969
and regional offices

Employment Appeal Tribunal
4 St James's Square
London SW1Y 4JU
01-210 3848

11 Melville Crescent
Edinburgh EH3 7LU
031-225 3963

Equal Opportunities Commission
Overseas House
Quay Street
Manchester M3 3HN
061-833 9244

Health and Safety Executive
Baynards House
Chepstow Place
Westbourne Grove
London W2 4TF
01-229 3456
and regional offices

Industrial Training Boards
Clothing and Allied Products
80 Richard Shaw Lane
Pudsey
Leeds LS28 6BN
0532 393355

Construction
Dewhurst House
24 West Smithfield
London EC1A 9JA
01-489 1662

Engineering
P O Box 176
54 Clarendon Road
Watford
Hertfordshire WD1 1LB
0923 38441

Hotel and Catering
International House
High Street
London W5 5DB
01-579 2400

Offshore Petroleum
Forties Road
Montrose
Angus DD10 9ET
0674 72230

Plastics Processing
Coppice House
Halesfield 7
Telford
Shropshire T7 4NA
0952 587020

Road Transport
Capitol House
Empire Way
Wembley
Middlesex HA9 0NG
01-902 8880

Industrial Tribunals
Central Office of the
Industrial Tribunals
93 Ebury Bridge Road
London SW1W 8RE
01-730 9161

Central Office of the
Industrial Tribunals
St Andrew House
141 West Nile Street
Glasgow G1 2RU
041-331 1601

Wages Inspectorate
Steel House
11 Tothill Street
London SW1H 9NF
01-213 3881

Index

add = address
ACAS 67, 92, 104, 113, 155, 163, 174; add 176
Accidents at work 121–3, 171
Advertising 12
Agricultural Wages Board 77, 164, add 177

Bankruptcy Act *1914* 64
Briefing groups 100

Central Arbitration Committee 92, 104, 157, add 177
Certificate of independence 91
Certification Officer 91, 163–4, add 177
Codes of practice 24, 29, 103, 114, 127, 162
Collective agreements 48
Commission for Racial Equality 24, 160, 161–2, add 177
Conciliation Officer 67
Confidential information 47
Consultants 14
Contracts:
 breaches 103, 143–4
 of employment 36–57
 entitlement 26
 fixed-term 38
 for services 40
 frustration 142
 open-ended 37–8
 particular purpose 38–40
 service agreements 39–40
 short-term 39
 specimen 50–55
 terms and conditions 37
 training 144

Dangerous occurrences 123–6
Data Protection Act 31, 162
Data Protection Registrar 162–3, add 177
Department of Employment 29, 154, 174–5, add 177
DHSS Inspector 72–73
Disabled Persons (Employment) Act *1944, 1958* 29
Disciplinary rules 44–5, 54–7, 75, 93
Disclosure of information 112
Discrimination 19–21, 23
Dismissal:
 constructive 144
 financial compensation 145–8
 lack of capability 133
 lack of qualifications 135
 long term sickness 134
 misconduct 136–7
 redundancy 137
 unfair 141–2
Driver's hours 172
DSS, *see* DHSS
Duties:
 employer 114–15
 general 108
 of employee 107–8
 of manufacturer/supplier 109
 other persons 108
Education (Work Experience) Act *1973* 25
Employee relations 91–105
Employing:
 children 25
 Commonwealth citizens 28
 Disabled persons 29, 172–3

EC nationals 28
Non-EC nationals 28–9
people with a criminal record 29–30
young persons 25–8, 173
Employment Acts *1980, 1988* 92, 95–6, 103
Employment agencies 13
Employment Appeal Tribunal 92, 152–3, 157, add 177
Employment Bill *1988* 25, 28, 44, 140, 145
Employment Medical Advisory Service 113
Employment Medical Advisory Services Act *1972* 26
Employment Protection Act *1975* 104, 163
Employment Protection (Consolidation) Act 1978 41, 59, 97
Equal Opportunities Commission 24, 160, add 177
Equal pay 66–7, 78–9
Equal Pay Act *1970* 67, 104, 160
Executive Search 14
Exit interviews 131

First aid 115
 boxes 118
 room 116
Forms required by law 169–73

Genuine occupational qualifications (GOQs) 22–3
Government bodies 154–65
Grievance procedures 54, 93

Head hunting 14
Health and safety 54–5, 57, 93, 106–28
 codes of practice 127–8
 legislation 127–8
 regulations 127
Health and Safety at Work Act (HASAWA) *1974, see* Health and safety
Health and Safety Commission 112, 158
Health and Safety Executive 112–13, 158, add 177
Health and Safety (First Aid) Regulations 114

Holidays 42
Hours of work 42

Identification 41
Induction 33–4
Industrial Training Act *1964* 159
Industrial Training Boards 159–60, add 177–8
Industrial tribunals 23–4, 37, 67, 69, 96, 133, 148, 156, add 178
 procedure 149–52
Insolvency 143
Interviews 15–19
Itemised pay statement 169

Jobcentres 29
Job evaluation 67, 78
Job offer 31

Market forces 78
Maternity:
 rights 60–63
 Statutory maternity pay (SMP) 61–2
Medical examination 31–2

National Insurance contributions 169–71
Notice 43–44, 129–33
Notices which employer must display 120–21
Notification of injuries 121

Occupational sick pay 73–4
Offer letter 32–3

Pay 76–90
 bonus 80
 internal relativities 77–8
 itemised statement 169
 piecework 80
 profit related 80
PAYE forms 83–90
Pensions 42–3, 47, 54, 64
Picketing 102–3

Race Relations Act *1976* 20, 22 24, 160
Records 34–5
Recruiting 9–35
Redundancy 137
 notifying the DOE 140
 pay 138–9
 rebates 140

time off 140
References 31
Rehabilitation 30
Rehabilitation of Offenders Act *1974* 30, 31
Rehabilitation of Offenders Act (Exceptions) (Amendments) Order *1986* 20
Remuneration 41
Reporting of accidents 121–3
Restraint of trade 48
Retirement 47, 143
Right of search 47

Safety:
  committee 100
  policies 114
  representative 113
Selection methods 19
Self-employed 10
Seven point plan 11
Sex Discrimination Act *1975* 20, 22, 24, 160
Short-time working 46
Social Security Acts *1975, 1985* 97
Specifications 11
Statutory maternity pay (SMP) 53–4, 61, 171–2
Statutory Minimum Wage 77
Statutory rights 58–75
  guarantee payments 58–9
  insolvency 64–5
  medical suspension pay 59
  public duties 63–4
  transfer of undertakings 65–6
Statutory sick pay (SSP) 42, 46, 51–2, 59, 68–75, 171
Strikes 103–4

continuous employment 105
  payment 105
Termination 54, 129–53
Terms and conditions:
  custom and practice 49
  implied 48–9
  negotiation of 93
  varying 49–50
  written 41–8
Training Agency 29, 158–9
Trade disputes 102–5
Trade Union Act *1980, 1988* 92, 102
Trade unions 65, 91
  membership 98
  recognition agreements 93–4, 98–9
  rights 97
  single union agreements 94, 96
Trade Union and Labour Relations Act (TULRA) *1974* 91, 103
Transfer of undertaking 65–7, 92, 97
Treaty of Rome 28

Unemployment initiatives 164–5
  job splitting 165
  training 165
  YTS 165

Wages 79
Wages Act *1986* 81, 164
Wages Council Act *1979* 164
Wages Councils 39, 76–7, 164, *add* 178
Work permit 28–9
Works committees 99–100
Written statement 41–48

Young Persons Employment Act *1938* 26
Youth Training Scheme 165